Strategies to Integrate the *Arts* in Mathematics

Authors

Linda Dacey, Ed.D.
Lisa Donovan, Ph.D.

 **Lesley** UNIVERSITY

 **SHELL EDUCATION**

Publishing Credits

Dona Herweck Rice, *Editor-in-Chief*; Robin Erickson, *Production Director*;
Lee Aucoin, *Creative Director*; Sara Johnson, M.S.Ed., *Editorial Director*;
Tracy Edmunds, *Editor*; Leah Quillian, *Assistant Editor*; Grace Alba, *Designer*;
Corinne Burton, M.A.Ed., *Publisher*

Contributing Authors

Louise Pascale, Ph.D., associate professor, Lesley University Creative Arts in Learning Division
Celeste Miller, M.F.A., adjunct faculty, Lesley University Creative Arts in Learning Division

Consultants

Jennifer Bogard, Doctoral Candidate, Lesley University and Literacy Coach
Devin Feirrera, music director, Charlestown Boys and Girls Club, Community Arts Master's Degree
     Candidate, Lesley University Creative Arts in Learning Division
Susan Griss, M.A., adjunct, Lesley University Creative Arts in Learning Division
Francine Jennings, Ed.D., national faculty, Lesley University Creative Arts in Learning Division
Jennifer Roosa, Grade 8 mathematics teacher, Lee Public Schools, MA
Carrie St. John, Grade 2 teacher, Lee Public Schools, MA

Image Credits
All images Shutterstock

Standards
© 2004 Mid-continent Research for Education and Learning (McREL)
© 2007 Teachers of English to Speakers of Other Languages, Inc. (TESOL)
© 2007 Board of Regents of the University of Wisconsin System. World-Class Instructional Design and Assessment
  (WIDA). For more information on using the WIDA ELP Standards, please visit the WIDA website at www.wida.us.
© 2010 National Governors Association Center for Best Practices and Council of Chief State School Officers (CCSS)

Shell Education

5301 Oceanus Drive
Huntington Beach, CA 92649-1030
http://www.shelleducation.com

ISBN 978-1-4258-1088-7

© 2013 Shell Educational Publishing, Inc.

Table of Contents

The Importance of Arts Integration

Teachers have an important and challenging job, and it seems that they are asked to do more with each passing year. We hear from teachers regularly that integrating the arts would be a great thing to do if they just had time and support from their administration. Yet research shows that integration of the arts is an efficient and effective strategy for addressing some of the greatest challenges in today's educational landscape as the arts deepen learning in ways that engage all learners of all abilities and needs (President's Committee on the Arts and the Humanities 2011; Burnaford 2007). Study after study points to compelling evidence of the significant outcomes that are linked to arts integration.

According to the President's Committee on the Arts and the Humanities, "studies have now documented significant links between arts integration models and academic and social outcomes for students, efficacy for teachers, and school-wide improvements in culture and climate. Arts integration is efficient, addressing a number of outcomes at the same time. Most important, the greatest gains in schools with arts integration are often seen school-wide and also with the most hard-to-reach and economically disadvantaged students" (2011).

A recent study funded by the Ford Foundation and led by researchers from Lesley University's Creative Arts in Learning Division and an external advisory team conducted research with over 200 alumni teaching across the country who had been trained in arts-integration strategies. The findings suggest that arts-integrated teaching provides a variety of strategies for accessing content and expressing understanding and creates learning that is culturally responsive and relevant in students' lives. This leads to deep learning, increased student ownership, and engagement with academic content. Not only does arts integration engage students in creativity, innovation, and imagination, it renews teachers' commitment to teaching (Bellisario and Donovan with Prendergast 2012).

Really then, the question becomes this: *How can we afford to not provide students with access to the arts as an engaging way to learn and to express ideas across the curriculum?*

Arts integration is the investigation of curricular content through artistic explorations where the arts provide an avenue for rigorous investigation, representation, expression, and reflection of both curricular content and the art form itself (Diaz, Donovan, and Pascale 2006). This series provides teachers with concrete strategies to integrate the arts across the curriculum with separate books for language arts, mathematics, social studies, and science. In each book, arts integration strategies are introduced with contextual information about the art form (creative movement, drama, music, poetry, storytelling, and visual arts).

The Importance of Arts Integration (*cont.*)

Each art form provides you with new ways to help students fully engage with content and participation in memorable learning experiences. Creative movement allows students to embody ideas and work conceptually. Drama challenges students to explore multiple perspectives of characters, historical figures, and scientists. Music develops students' ability to listen, to generate a sense of community, and to communicate and connect aurally. Poetry invites students to build a more playful, fresh relationship to written and spoken language. Storytelling connects us with our roots in the oral tradition and heightens our awareness of the role stories play in our lives. Visual art taps into our ability to observe critically, to envision, to think through metaphor, and to build visual literacy in a world where images are pervasive.

Providing learners with the opportunity to investigate concepts and to express their understanding with the powerful languages of the arts will deepen students' understanding, heighten their curiosity, and bring forward their voices as they interact more fully with content and translate their ideas into new forms. This book is a beginning, a "way in."

We invite you to see for yourself by bringing the strategies shared in this book to your classroom and see what happens. We hope this resource leaves you looking for deeper experiences with the arts for both you and your students.

What Does It Mean to Integrate the Arts?

When am I ever going to use this? No doubt, nearly all math teachers have heard these words and perhaps even uttered them at some point. For the majority of learners, the idea that what they are learning will be useful later, whether for college, work, or life, is simply not enough. Samuel Otten (2011) suggests that a better approach to teaching mathematics would be to establish a learning environment in which "students are happily engaged in learning mathematics and unlikely to challenge its purpose (e.g., students are finding intrinsic value in mathematical discovery and sense making)" (24). We believe that a vital element necessary in establishing such a learning environment can be found in the integration of math and the arts because active involvement in the arts can help learners explore different perspectives and internalize new ideas and ways of thinking.

Mathematics is too often taught in a rote manner, ignoring its beauty. "Instead of teaching mathematics as the mere manipulations of numbers, lines, and algorithms, it is both important and possible to bring the beauty of mathematics into the classroom" (Nascimento and Barco 2007, 69). When we integrate mathematics into the arts, learning activities become multisensory, gain relevance, and add joy to the learning experience. The arts provide a vivid and dynamic context within which learners can wrestle with mathematical ideas, test conjectures, and hone their mathematical reasoning.

The Importance of Arts Integration (cont.)

Interestingly, arts integration is most likely to happen in subjects other than mathematics (Catterall and Waldorf 1999). This happens, in part, because of how our society too often attributes an aura of mystique to these two bodies of knowledge. Many of us conclude that both of these areas belong to the few who have been given special gifts, who have rare expertise. But you don't need to be an artist or a mathematician to add this teaching approach to your repertoire. We cannot emphasize this point enough. No special abilities or talents are needed except for the willingness to try!

Most of us recognize that there are many connections between the arts and mathematics, particularly in the visual arts and music. For example, architects, sculptors, and musicians rely on mathematical knowledge every day. And there are times in the mathematics classroom when the arts are used to introduce or culminate the study of a mathematical topic. Many teachers may have favorite lessons in which quilts, tessellations, or the golden rectangle are explored. What we are aiming for here, though, is a seamless blending of the two areas in a sustained manner where experience and knowledge in both disciplines is enhanced. We will make it possible for you to teach lessons in which the arts provide a context in which mathematical ideas take shape and deepen while the arts inform and enrich the lives of students. We don't want you to do this in a tangential manner or on an enrichment basis. Rather, we want you to use arts integration as an approach to teaching the most prevalent standards in your mathematics curriculum and to do so frequently. In teaching mathematical ideas through artistic explorations, students will develop skills and knowledge in both disciplines. So we will share strategies with you that are flexible enough to be used across content strands and grade levels.

Why Should I Integrate the Arts?

Mathematics along with reading continues to dominate classroom instruction and mandated assessments. Government-led initiatives such as the Common Core State Standards and the No Child Left Behind Act focus nearly exclusively on these two subjects. International achievement gaps in mathematics have narrowed with all of this attention but continue to exist. Significant gaps also continue to exist between students within the United States in relation to minority status and poverty. Mathematical knowledge is critical to the success of our students. Something needs to change.

With our curriculum dominated by reading and mathematics, little room is left for the arts. Yet as educators, we want to teach the whole child. Students need both the arts and academic disciplines. Research suggests that academic achievement may be linked to the arts (Kennedy 2006). As noted by Douglas Reeves (2007), "the challenge for school leaders is to offer every student a rich experience with the arts without sacrificing the academic opportunities students need" (80). By integrating the arts with mathematics, we are able to place mathematical ideas within rich settings *and* provide our students with access to the arts. In fact, the arts can lead to "deep learning" (Bellisario and Donovan with Prendergast 2012) where students are more genuinely engaged with academic content, spend more time on task, and take ownership of their learning while deepening their imaginative and creative skills.

The Importance of Arts Integration *(cont.)*

Mathematics and science are frequently linked together in schools, with STEM (Science, Technology, Engineering, and Mathematics) initiatives formalizing this association. However, for some students, connecting math to science only serves to make math less accessible. While we applaud STEM efforts, we seek to expand the potential for other interdisciplinary connections. The arts also offer particular advantages for learning that should not be ignored. In a briefing on changing STEM to STEAM with the inclusion of the arts, John Maeda, president of the Rhode Island School of Design, noted that STEM would benefit by adding the arts and design to trigger more innovation (Rhode Island School of Design 2011). Beth Baker (2012) states that "innovation happens through science, technology, engineering and mathematics. Could it be missing something that is actually quite important? It's missing the arts—the right-brain innovation that has propelled our country, made us competitive" (253).

Rinne et al. (2011) identify several ways in which arts integration improves long-term retention through elaboration, enactment, and rehearsal. Specifically, when learners create and add details to their own visual models, dramatize a concept or skill, sing a song repeatedly, or rehearse for a performance, they are increasing the likelihood that they will remember what they have learned. This retention lasts not just for the next chapter test but over significant periods of time. Through repetition that doesn't feel like drill and kill, this information is retained for life because students become deeply engaged when working in arts integration. They eagerly revisit, review, rehearse, edit, and work through ideas repeatedly in authentic ways as they translate ideas into new forms.

As brain research deepens our understanding of how learning takes place, educators have come to better appreciate the importance of the arts. The arts support communication, emotional connections, community, and higher-order thinking. They are also linked to increased academic achievement, especially among at-risk students. Eric Jensen (2001) argues that the "arts enhance the process of learning. The systems they nourish, which include our integrated sensory, attentional, cognitive, emotional, and motor capabilities, are, in fact, the driving forces behind all other learning." Lessons and activities that integrate mathematics and the arts provide a rich environment for the exploration of mathematical ideas for all students, but particularly for those students who need new ways to access curriculum and to express understanding. Integrated math and arts lessons can also motivate students.

The Center for Applied Special Technology (http://www.cast.org/about/index.html) suggests that in meeting the needs of variable learners, educators should expand their teaching to provide universal design. That is, that teachers include strategies that "are flexible and responsive to the needs of all learners" by providing "multiple means of engagement, methods of presentation of content, and multiple avenues for expression of understanding." The integration of the arts provides opportunities to address universal design principles.

Arts and the Standards

Connections to the Common Core State Standards for Mathematical Practice

Within the Common Core State Standards for Mathematics are the eight Standards for Mathematical Practices (National Governors Association Center for Best Practices and Council of Chief State School Officers 2011):

1. Make sense of problems and persevere in solving them
2. Reason abstractly and quantitatively
3. Construct viable arguments and critique the reasoning of others
4. Model with mathematics
5. Use appropriate tools strategically
6. Attend to precision
7. Look for and make use of structure
8. Look for and express regularity in repeated reasoning

These practices are intended to be interwoven with the content standards and can be thought of as the mathematical habits of mind that students need to develop. Sense making, communication, perseverance, and representation are prominent in these standards. As students represent mathematical ideas in artistic forms, they are involved in interpreting or making sense of ideas. The creation of related artistic products also engages students' interest, provides contexts for math, and encourages perseverance as students translate ideas into new forms. Thus, these lessons strengthen students' expertise in these standards and help learners actively engage in making mathematical ideas meaningful.

Artistic Habits of Mind

As well as mathematical habits of mind, students will also be developing artistic habits of mind (Hetland et al. 2007). With these habits of mind, students are able to:

1. Develop craft
2. Engage and persist
3. Envision
4. Express
5. Observe
6. Reflect
7. Stretch and explore
8. Understand the art world

Though these habits were identified in an investigation of visual art practices, they are relevant for the practice of all of the arts.

It is important to note that the skills that are a significant part of what the arts develop are valued in every field. The arts develop these skills naturally as students explore and translate ideas into artistic form. Researcher Lois Hetland notes that "it is these qualities—intrinsic to the arts—that are valued in every domain but not necessarily taught in those subjects in school. That's what makes the arts such potent resources for teaching valued dispositions—what the arts teach well is not used uniquely in the arts but is valuable across a wide spectrum of contexts" (2009, 37).

Arts and the Standards (cont.)

Classroom Environment

A safe classroom environment is needed for mathematical ideas and artistic expressions to flourish. Learners must feel comfortable to make mistakes, to critique the work of others, and to celebrate success. Think back to groups to which you have presented new ideas or creative works. How did you feel as you waited for their reactions? What was it about their behavior that made you feel more or less comfortable? What was it about your thinking that made you feel more or less safe? Such reflections will lead you to ways in which you can talk about these ideas with your students. As teachers, we must be role models for our students as we model our willingness to take risks and engage in new ways of learning. You will find that the arts by their nature invite risk taking, experimentation, and self-discipline as well as encourage the development of a supportive learning community.

Developing a learning community in which learners support and respect one another takes time, but there are things that you can do to help support its development:

- **Establish clear expectations for respect.** Respect is nonnegotiable. As students engage in creative explorations, it is crucial that they honor one another's ideas, invite all voices to the table, and discuss the work in ways that value each contribution. Self-discipline and appreciation for fellow students' creative work is often a beneficial outcome of arts integration (Bellisario and Donovan with Prendergast 2012). Take time for students to brainstorm ways in which they can show one another respect and what they can do when they feel that they have not been respected. Work with students to create guidelines for supporting the creative ideas of others and agree to uphold them as a group.

- **Explore several icebreakers** during the first weeks of school that allow students to get to know one another informally and begin to discover interests they have in common. As students learn more about one another, they develop a sense of themselves as individuals and as a classroom unit and are more apt to want to support one another. Using fun, dynamic warm-ups not only helps students get their brains working but also builds a sense of community and support for risk taking.

- **Tell your students about ways in which you are engaged in learning new ideas.** Talk about your realizations and challenges along the way, and demonstrate your own willingness to take risks and persevere.

Arts and the Standards *(cont.)*

- **Find ways to support the idea that we can all act, draw, sing, rhyme, and so forth.** Avoid saying negative things about your own arts or math skill levels, and emphasize your continuous growth.

- **Learn to ask questions rather than give answers.** By asking a question like, "What does this symbol represent to you?," students are able to focus or clarify their own thinking.

- **Avoid judgments.** Students who are trying to earn your praise for their artistic products will not take the risks necessary for creative work. Encourage students to reflect on their own goals and whether they think they have met them.

- **Emphasize process over product.** Enormous learning and discovery take place during the creative process. This is as significant as the final product that is produced, and in some cases even more so.

How This Book Is Organized

Strategies

The strategies and lesson ideas in this book are organized within six art modalities:

- creative movement

- drama

- music

- poetry

- storytelling

- visual arts

Within each modality, five strategies are presented that integrate that art form into the teaching of mathematics. The strategies are not intended as an exhaustive list but rather as exemplary ways to integrate the arts into mathematics.

Though we have provided a model lesson for each strategy, these strategies are flexible and can be used in a number of ways across a variety of content areas. These models will allow you to try out the ideas with your students and to envision many other ways to adapt these strategies for use in your teaching. For example, we emphasized shapes in our drama strategy of monologues, but you may prefer to integrate the arts into other areas of mathematics, such as the four basic operations or specific classifications of numbers (fractions, decimals, negatives). Also note that strategies can be implemented across the art forms. For example, the strategy of juxtaposition could be associated with any of the arts, as we can juxtapose movements, characters, sounds, words, perspectives, or materials. Furthermore, as you become more familiar and comfortable with the strategies, you can combine a variety of them across the art modalities within one lesson. For example, you might have students begin with creative movement to explore shapes, then dramatize experts in the field finding examples of shapes and listing the terms and characteristics they associate with those shapes, and finally, use those words as a resource of "found words" to write a poem. The goal is to make the choices that best fit you and your students.

How This Book Is Organized (cont.)

Organization of the Lessons

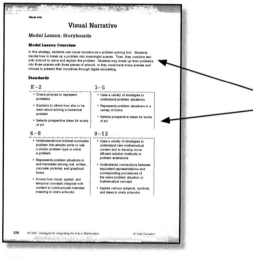

Each model lesson begins with an **overview**, followed by the list of **standards** addressed. Note that the standards involve equal rigor for both mathematics and the arts.

A list of **materials** you will need is provided.

A **preparation** section follows in which ways you can better ensure a successful learning investigation have been identified. Ideas may relate to grouping students, using props to engage learners, or practicing readings with dramatic flair.

The **procedure** section provides step-by-step directions on how to implement the model lesson.

Each model lesson includes **questions** that you can ask as students work. The questions serve to highlight students' mathematical reasoning, stimulate their artistic thinking, or debrief their experience.

How This Book Is Organized (*cont.*)

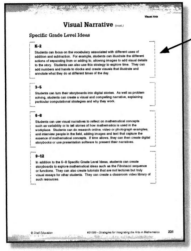

Specific grade level ideas follow with suggestions on how to better meet the needs of students within the K–2, 3–5, 6–8, and 9–12 grade levels. They may also suggest other ways to explore or extend the ideas in the model lesson at these levels. Read all of the sections, as an idea written for a different grade span may suggest something you want to do with your students.

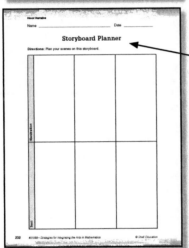

At least one **reproducible** is provided for each model lesson. Often in the form of graphic organizers, the reproducibles are designed to help students brainstorm ideas, organize and record their thinking, or reflect on their learning. Reproducibles are available on the Digital Resource CD in PDF form and oftentimes as Word documents to allow for customization of content and text for students of diverse abilities and needs.

How This Book Is Organized (cont.)

How to Use the Lessons

These strategies can be used to teach mathematics in any K–12 classroom with any mathematics curriculum. A strategy lesson can be implemented as a lesson for a day, or, if you have the flexibility, expanded to several days or a week. You may choose to use the strategy lesson within your mathematics lesson or in combination with time assigned to the arts or, when considering storytelling or poetry, perhaps in conjunction with language arts periods.

You may wish to focus on one art form at a time to help yourself become familiar with using that art modality to teach mathematics. Or you may want to look through the content index and explore models that relate to what you are teaching now or are about to teach. Over time, you will become familiar with the strategies and find that you choose to integrate them on a regular basis. If integrating arts and mathematics is new to you, consider working with another teacher to explore the ideas together. Think about collaborating with art, dance, drama, or music teachers in your school system to draw from their expertise in deepening the artistic work.

Assessment

Data-driven decision making, documentation of learning, and meeting benchmarks are all phrases referring to assessment practices that permeate our schools. Assessment has become a time-consuming activity for all involved in education, and yet the time and effort spent does not always yield what is needed to improve learning. As you think about how to assess lessons and activities that integrate math and the arts, it's important to stop and consider how to best use assessment to increase learning for your students. It is most likely that in addressing that goal, you will also be documenting learning in ways that can be shared with students, families, administrators, and other interested stakeholders.

We encourage you to focus on formative assessment; that is, assessment that is incorporated throughout the process of learning. This assessment will inform your instructional decisions during the process of teaching. The purpose of this assessment is to provide feedback for learners and teachers along the way in addition to assessment of learning at the end. As such, we are equally as interested in the data collected during the learning process as well as after it is completed. The goals are to make the learning process visible, to determine the depth of understanding, and to note the process the students undergo as they translate their mathematical knowledge into an art form or explore mathematical ideas through artistic explorations.

How This Book Is Organized *(cont.)*

There are a variety of tools you can use to gather data to support your instructional decision making:

- **Ask questions to draw out, clarify, and probe students' thinking.** The questions in each strategy section will provide you with ideas on which you can elaborate. Use questioning to make on-the-spot adjustments to your plans as well as to identify learning moments as they unfold. This can be as simple as posing a new question or as complex as bringing a few students together for a mini-lesson.

- **Walk around with a clipboard or notebook** so that you can easily capture student comments and questions as well as your own observations. Too often, we think we will remember students' words only to find ourselves unable to reproduce them at a later time. These annotations will allow you to note patterns within a student's remarks or among students' comments. They can suggest misconceptions that provide you with an entry to the next day's work through a comment such as, "Yesterday, I heard a few of you say that you drew a square instead of a rectangle. Let's talk about what that means." A suggested template is provided in Appendix B (page 271). Make several copies and attach them to a clipboard.

- **Use the graphic organizers in the strategy sections** as support for the creative process. Using these forms, have students brainstorm ideas for their art product and their mathematical connections. These organizers provide a snapshot of the students' thinking at a point in the creative process.

- **Use a camera to document student learning.** Each of the strategies leads to a creative product but not necessarily one that provides a tangible artifact or one that fits on a standard size piece of paper. Use a digital camera to take numerous pictures that can capture, for example, a piece of visual art at various stages of development or the gestures actors and storytellers use in their dramatic presentations. Similarly, use video to capture planning sessions, group discussions, and final presentations. As well as documenting learning, collecting such evidence helps students reflect back on their learning. Consider developing a learning portfolio for your students that they can review and compile over time.

How This Book Is Organized *(cont.)*

- Recognize that although each strategy leads to a final creative product, it, too, can be used to inform future instruction. **Comparisons can be made across products to note student growth.**

- **Make students integral parts of the assessment process.** Provide them with opportunities to reflect on their work. For quick, formative reflections, ask students to respond simply; for example, say, "Hold up one to four fingers to show me how well you think you represented math ideas in your picture." Have students reflect in more complex ways as well; for example, have students choose artifacts to include in their portfolio and explain the reasons for their choices. Have students reflect on their work as a class; for example, ask, "How well did we build on one another's mathematical ideas today? How well did we support one another's creative thinking?" Encourage discussion of artistic work to draw out not only what students have learned in their own creative process, but also how and what they learn from the work of their peers. In this way, students teach and learn from one another.

- **Design rubrics that help you organize your assessment data.** A well-crafted rubric can help you gather data more quickly as well as increase the likelihood that you are being equitable in your evaluation of assessment data. Select criteria to assess learning in mathematics as well as in the art form because arts integration supports equal rigor in both content and in the arts.

To give you an example of how you might combine these methods, we will consider the Exaggeration strategy in Storytelling. In the model lesson for this strategy, the teacher tells the students a trickster tale in which the sly fox tricks other animals out of their money by suggesting, for example, that two quarters would be better than a dollar bill that can easily rip and burn. In the first part of the lesson, students engage with the story by using gestures that model the behavior of the other characters in the story. A photograph of the students can document them in their roles. Next, students are asked to create their own stories. The graphic organizers students use provide a record of their initial thinking.

How This Book Is Organized (*cont.*)

Students then create their own trickster tales, which are recorded for documentation purposes. In Carrie St. John's classroom at Lee Elementary School in Lee, Massachusetts, students also wanted to write their stories. The variation in the stories demonstrates the wide range of learners in this second-grade classroom that is made more apparent because of the open-ended nature of the task. Some students provide one scenario in their stories while some include several "tricks." Some of the stories replicate the exchanges in the original story while others create quite different exchanges. The variation in the amount of mathematical detail included in the stories is quite notable. In their telling of the stories, students demonstrated their different abilities to capture the characters through voice, gestures, and stance. Students' use of language varies greatly as well. Also, it is interesting to note students who are stronger in their storytelling than in the development of the mathematical ideas, or vice versa. Noting such differences can inform your planning for instructional focus and grouping decisions. Most important is the teacher's reflection that these students were excited to create and tell their stories, and that their use of language was more creative and descriptive than they had demonstrated previously.

Consider these excerpts from students' stories:

Dylan provided an interesting introduction to his story, establishing the setting, character, and plot. He set himself apart by choosing a trickster that was not an animal:

> *Once upon a time, in fact it was just a couple of hours ago, there was a tiny green leprechaun named Lucky. He lived in Ireland and was known far and wide for being a trickster! Lucky was enthusiastic when it came to his pranks, but he had a big problem. Lucky lived on a magic rainbow that could only be unlocked if you paid the mystery amount. Lucky only had 3 nickels, and he was sick of being broke. "What's a leprechaun to do with only 3 nickels?" he asked himself. "Hmmmm, I need a good trick to play!"*

The actual tricks in the story involved trading a big nickel for a small dime, an exchange that was repeated three times.

Hayden and Maya provided four different exchanges in their story and gave detailed mathematical information about each trade:

> *Fish said, "Thanks!" Now pig had 10 cents. It costs 1 dollar to get into the game. He needs 90 more cents. Next, he saw octopus. Octopus had 15 pennies. Pig said to him, "I'll give you this one, light dime for all those heavy pennies. This will be much easier for you to carry to the game."*

How This Book Is Organized (*cont.*)

Pig then tricks a seahorse, an octopus, and a stingray before meeting up with a whale. Note the vivid imagery and humor at the end of this story:

> *She [whale] sneezed and the water wooshed and splashed like a tidal wave. Pig's dollar flew out of his hand and right back to whale. And then whale said, "Hey, aren't you a pig? You shouldn't be underwater anyways!"*

Madison did not have his trickster lose the money at the end, but he did capture the motivation for learning mathematics. Note this section at the end of his story:

> *So snake got to go to the beach, and dog couldn't go. When dog tried to get in, he found out that he had less money than before. He was sad that snake tricked him. He didn't want to get tricked again, so now he's going to learn to count money.*

As there are so many aspects of this task to capture, a rubric can be quite helpful. A suggested rubric is provided in Appendix B (page 272). Observation protocols help teachers document evidence of student learning, something all teachers must do. A variety of forms could be used, and it's not possible to include all areas that you might attend to in an interdisciplinary lesson. Two suggested forms are included in Appendix B, built on the work of Collins (2012a, 2012b) and Dacey (2012a, 2012b, 2012c, 2012d). One form is for use with individual students (page 273), and one for use with groups (page 274).

Correlation to the Standards

Shell Education is committed to producing educational materials that are research and standards based. In this effort, we have correlated all of our products to the academic standards of all 50 United States, the District of Columbia, the Department of Defense Dependent Schools, and all Canadian provinces.

How to Find Standards Correlations

To print a customized correlation report of this product for your state, visit our website at http://www.shelleducation.com and follow the on-screen directions. If you require assistance in printing correlation reports, please contact Customer Service at 1-877-777-3450.

Purpose and Intent of Standards

Legislation mandates that all states adopt academic standards that identify the skills students will learn in kindergarten through grade twelve. Many states also have standards for Pre-K. This same legislation sets requirements to ensure the standards are detailed and comprehensive.

Standards are designed to focus instruction and guide adoption of curricula. Standards are statements that describe the criteria necessary for students to meet specific academic goals. They define the knowledge, skills, and content students should acquire at each level. Standards are also used to develop standardized tests to evaluate students' academic progress. Teachers are required to demonstrate how their lessons meet state standards. State standards are used in the development of all of our products, so educators can be assured they meet the academic requirements of each state.

Common Core State Standards

The lessons in this book are aligned to the Common Core State Standards (CCSS). The standards support the objectives presented throughout the lessons and are provided on the Digital Resource CD (standards.pdf).

McREL Compendium

We use the Mid-continent Research for Education and Learning (McREL) Compendium to create standards correlations. Each year, McREL analyzes state standards and revises the compendium. By following this procedure, McREL is able to produce a general compilation of national standards. Each lesson in this product is based on one or more McREL standards, which are also provided on the Digital Resource CD (standards.pdf).

TESOL and WIDA Standards

The lessons in this book promote English language development for English language learners. The standards correlations can be found on the Digital Resource CD (standards.pdf).

Correlation to the Standards (cont.)

The main focus of the lessons presented in this book is to promote the integration of the arts in mathematics. The standards for both the arts and mathematics are provided on the Digital Resource CD (standards.pdf).

Common Core State Standards

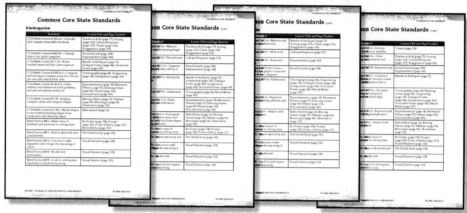

McREL Standards

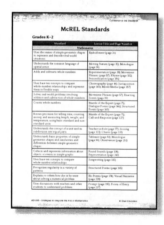

TESOL and WIDA Standards

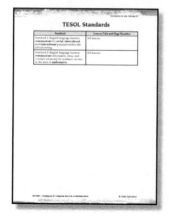
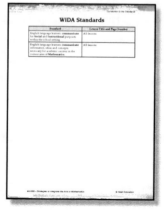

Creative Movement

#51088—Strategies to Integrate the Arts in Mathematics

Creative Movement

Understanding Creative Movement

Integrating creative movement across the curriculum is an engaging approach to learning that allows students to experience, translate, and communicate mathematical ideas kinesthetically. In 1983, Howard Gardner identified bodily-kinesthetic intelligence within his theory of multiple intelligences (2011) as one way that students learn. Neuroscientists are finding that memory and recall is improved when the body is engaged in the learning process (Zull 2002) and that the mind uses the body to make sense of ideas (Carpenter 2010).

While important for all learners, opportunities to express themselves nonverbally can be particularly powerful to strengthen students' linguistic skills. Such opportunities can provide students with access to mathematical content that would not be possible otherwise. Stacey Skoning (2008) states that creative movement, or dance, "is important to incorporate into our inclusive classrooms if we want to meet the needs of more diverse groups of students."

Creative movement allows students to be physically active, which often increases students' attention span, but it's much more than just the incorporation of movement into classroom activities. When students are involved in creative movement, they become more mindful of their bodies' ability to communicate, explore what happens when they move with intention, engage in problem solving through movement, and develop awareness of their creative choices. It's important to keep the possibilities for this work in mind as your students explore these lessons.

As students deconstruct and reconstruct concepts, they take ownership of the ideas through kinesthetic means and creative choices. When students translate mathematical ideas into movement, they create meaning for abstract ideas and, through the process, they gain a more positive attitude toward mathematics (Werner 2001).

Creative Movement (cont.)

Strategies for Creative Movement

✇ Embodiment

In this strategy, students use shapes (body shapes, lines, angles, curves), level (low, middle, high), and movement or gesture to *embody*, or show with their bodies, their understanding of concepts and terms. The strategy can be used to model complex ideas, helping students to grasp, investigate, and internalize concepts. Students can also create spontaneous creative movement to help them summarize or review their learning.

Working with others to embody ideas in movement can prompt students to discuss characteristics of a particular concept, both as they translate ideas into movement and while they view the presentation of other groups' ideas. Dance artist Celeste Miller suggests that the language of movement can provide a "palette for expression of both abstract and tangible ideas" (Miller, pers. comm. 2012). Having groups of students embody the same concept allows these students to see how different movement interpretations can convey the same ideas. Coming up with more than one approach for depicting an idea encourages creative and critical thinking. This strategy can help students solidify ideas and help you assess students' depth of understanding.

✇ Moving Statues

This strategy combines held poses with movement as students incorporate the use of shape (body shapes, lines, angles, curves), level (low, medium, high), and quality of movement (characteristics such as sustained, swing, percussive, collapsed), allowing them to make nuanced changes in movement. Students can form moving statues alone, in pairs, or in groups.

A group statue results in a large, fluid representation of a concept as students create an evolving model of the idea being explored. Moving statues also can require students to position themselves in relationship to others. Through such experiences, creative movement can improve self-esteem and social functioning (Theodorakou and Zervas 2003).

✇ Experimentation

In this strategy, students use physical problem solving to discover new knowledge. As they explore curricular topics, students embody ideas and investigate them through movement, triggering new ways of thinking and allowing for generalizations to be discovered. For the process to truly be experimental, concepts should be considered before they are fully developed. Coaching students through cues and open-ended questions will improve their critical thinking and creative choices (Chen 2001). Experimentation can also be used to introduce a new topic and need not take a long time.

Creative Movement (cont.)

❧ Choreography

Audiences can be mesmerized by dancers moving across the stage, alone, in pairs, or in groups. Dancers can seem to move seamlessly from individual locations as they join together as a group and then part to return to individual spots. Choreographers orchestrate this motion through the planning and notation of movement.

Choreography requires students to decide how to incorporate moves, pathways, tempo, and location into a creative movement piece and then to notate or communicate those decisions. Without such notation, dance instructions could not be transmitted over time (Waters and Gibbons 2004).

❧ Movement Phrases

In this strategy, students create a series of movements to represent the parts of a process or concept. They perform this series of movements, linking each to the next to illustrate a series of steps or components within a curricular concept. When students link ideas, they can better understand relationships among concepts and form generalizations. As students create and build upon their movement ideas, they also develop the vocabulary of movement, such as directional words (pathways) and levels (high, medium, low). According to Stacey Skoning (2008), "having a common movement vocabulary in the classroom benefits everyone because the common vocabulary makes it easier to discuss the movement phrases that are being created."

Embodiment

Model Lesson: Vocabulary

Model Lesson Overview

Students use embodied movement to review mathematical vocabulary and concepts at the close of a lesson or unit or during a review session. Students work in groups to physically explore and show their understanding of mathematical terms and concepts through movement and share their ideas with the class.

Standards

K–2

- Uses the names of simple geometric shapes to represent and describe real-world situations
- Moves his or her body in a variety of controlled ways
- Creates shapes at low, middle, and high levels (different heights from the floor)

3–5

- Knows basic geometric language for describing and naming shapes
- Creates shapes at low, middle, and high levels (different heights from the floor)
- Uses kinesthetic awareness, concentration, and focus in performing movement skills

6–8

- Understands the defining properties of three-dimensional figures
- Understands various movements and their underlying principles

9–12

- Understands and applies basic and advanced properties of the concepts of geometry
- Uses appropriate skeletal alignment, body-part articulation, strength, flexibility, agility, and coordination in locomotor and nonlocomotor/axial movements

Materials

- *Embodied Movement Brainstorming Guide* (page 30, embrainstormingguide.pdf)
- *Embodied Movement Observation Recording Chart* (page 31, emrecordingchart.pdf)

Embodiment *(cont.)*

Preparation

Decide on the mathematical vocabulary you would like students to embody through movement. Compile a list of possible terms or phrases that might be investigated so that you can add them to ideas students suggest. The Specific Grade Level Ideas that accompany this lesson provide specific ideas, and curricular guides are also a good source of vocabulary words. An initial exploration with geometric shapes is suggested; identify another term or phrase if this is not appropriate for your students. Think about what size student groupings will be most productive for creating these embodied representations.

Procedure

1. Model the embodiment strategy with the whole class by playing a game called "Answer Me In Movement." Tell students that you are going to name a mathematical term or phrase and they are going to respond by using their bodies to create shapes or movements to show their understanding of the term. For example, say, "Triangle," and then say, "Answer me in movement." Encourage students to show different directions for the lines to portray them in as many ways as possible. Have students compare and contrast the different embodiments.

2. Distribute the *Embodied Movement Brainstorming Guide* (page 30) to students. Have students brainstorm other terms or phrases in the lesson or unit to embody through movement. Have students record their ideas along with notes about the mathematical idea and ways to represent it through creative movement.

3. Have students break into small groups and choose one of the terms from the *Embodied Movement Brainstorming Guide* to embody through movement as a group. Encourage students to choose a term that they find challenging to remember or would like to understand more fully. Explain that they must find a way to combine their bodies together as they express the concept using shape (round, straight and narrow, straight and wide, twisted, etc.), level (low, middle, high), and movement. Tell groups that they should not share their chosen term outside their group so that when they present their embodied movement, their classmates can identify the concept being represented.

4. As students work, check in with each group to provide encouragement and ask questions to deepen conceptual development. In some cases, students may use a symbolic gesture such as holding up their hands in the form of the addition sign. Encourage students to move beyond iconic symbols and to explore the meaning of the idea through movement.

Embodiment *(cont.)*

5. Have each group present their embodied movement to the rest of the class twice so that the audience has time to take in the details. The viewers can note their observations on the *Embodied Movement Observation Recording Chart* (page 31). Ask viewing students to use their observations to help them identify the term or phrase represented. Use viewer observations as a catalyst to spark conversations about the ideas represented.

6. Use the Questions for Discussion to prompt students' reflections on how they translated ideas into movement and what they saw in other groups' embodiments that suggested a particular mathematical term.

Questions for Discussion

- What came up in your discussion about how to translate a mathematical idea into movement?

- What math did you need to know about the term or phrase in order to translate it into movement?

- What struck you about other groups' presentations?

- What mathematical ideas were demonstrated?

- What movement elements were used?

Specific Grade Level Ideas

K–2

Record students' brainstorming ideas on chart paper rather than have them use the *Embodied Movement Brainstorming Guide*. Have students focus on one term at a time. Following the presentation of embodied ideas, work with students as a group to document their observations on the *Embodied Movement Observation Recording Chart*. Suggested vocabulary words to be embodied include names of shapes, comparative terms (e.g., *more, fewer*), and words associated with addition and subtraction.

3–5

The activity can be used as written. In addition to the names of shapes, students can embody a variety of geometric terms such as those used to classify angles and lines and those associated with the coordinate plane. Terms related to multiplication, division, and fractions can also be explored.

Embodiment *(cont.)*

6–8

Students can use the *Embodied Movement Brainstorming Guide* to individually brainstorm a complete list of vocabulary words related to three-dimensional figures. Then, in small groups of three or four, have students share their lists, jointly deciding on three words to embody. Examples of geometric terms to be embodied include *prism*, *vertex*, *net*, *surface area*, and *volume*. Additionally, terms related to proportional reasoning, types of numbers, and statistics and probability are appropriate for this activity. Discuss how certain elements of movement such as alignment, balance, and weight shift are used to embody these terms.

9–12

Students can use the *Embodied Movement Brainstorming Guide* to individually brainstorm a complete list of vocabulary words related to three-dimensional figures. Then, in small groups of three or four, have students share their lists, jointly deciding on three words to embody. Examples of geometric terms to be embodied include *arc*, *chord*, and *tangent*. In addition to geometric terms and those related to statistics and probability, students can embody terms related to functions. Have students work in groups to create more complex embodiments such as the lower bound of a parabola. Discuss how strength, flexibility, agility, and coordination are used to embody these terms.

Name _____ Date _____

Embodied Movement
Brainstorming Guide

Directions: Brainstorm mathematical words or ideas and write them in the *Word* column. Write characteristics of each in the *Math Characteristics* column and possible movements that show those characteristics in the *Movement Ideas* column.

Movement Ideas										
Math Characteristics										
Word										

Name _____ Date _____

Embodied Movement Observation Recording Chart

Directions: As you watch each group perform, record your observations and questions on the chart.

Group Members	What Movements Did You Observe?	What Mathematical Ideas Did You Observe?	What Questions Do You Have for the Performers?

Moving Statues

Model Lesson: Mirror Math

Model Lesson Overview

Moving statues can be used to represent a variety of mathematical concepts and relationships. The focus is on symmetry and reflection. Students begin with axial movements (movements made while stationary in place) and then explore locomotor movements (movements made from place to place). When students join a moving statue, they must decide how their levels, shapes, and movements can fit with the symmetry that the group has already established.

Standards

K–2

- Understands the common language of spatial sense
- Uses basic nonlocomotor/axial movements
- Uses locomotor movements in different directions

3–5

- Understands basic properties of figures
- Uses basic nonlocomotor/axial movements
- Uses locomotor movements in different directions

6–8

- Understands geometric transformations of figures
- Transfers a spatial pattern from the visual to the kinesthetic

Materials

- *Mirror Moves* (page 37, mirrormoves.pdf)
- Music *(optional)*

Moving Statues *(cont.)*

Preparation

Think about your students' comfort levels. Should they begin sitting in their chairs, or can they begin standing? Identify how pairs and small groups will be formed: through choice, through a random process such as matching cards, or assigned by you. Also identify music, if you wish to use it. A slow tempo is recommended. Other ideas are provided in the Specific Grade Level Ideas.

Procedure

1. Invite students to make some axial movements (movements made while staying rooted in one place) with their arms. Then, have students identify how they moved one arm in comparison to the other (e.g., at the same or different times, one on each side or both on the same side, the same or different movements, the same or different speeds).

2. Direct students to imagine a vertical line down the middle of their bodies. Ask them to move their arms so that each side of their bodies looks exactly the same. Invite students to imagine a drawing of themselves. Ask them to determine where they could fold the drawing so that the two sides matched exactly on top of each other. Have students indicate this midline on their bodies. Introduce or review the concept of symmetry.

3. Have students make axial arm movements. Then call "freeze," and have students lock into whatever position they are in, like a statue. Unfreeze a few students and ask them to indicate which student "statues" are symmetric and which are not. Introduce the term *asymmetric* to describe those that are not. Repeat the activity several times.

4. Divide students into pairs and have them face each other. Tell students they will take turns leading and following as they create a symmetrical "moving statue." The leader should make slow axial movements, and the follower should mirror the leader's movements as closely as possible. Students should not touch. Ask a pair to demonstrate the roles. Point out the plane of symmetry between the students.

5. Have pairs of students scatter about the room and decide who will lead first. Tell each pair to leave enough space between themselves and other pairs to be able to move without touching another group. Tell students that their movements should be axial (stay in one place). Encourage them to think intentionally about the different ways they could move, perhaps thinking of themselves as blades of grass blowing in the wind or as robots trying to dance. Encourage students to move in slow motion so that the movements look as if they are happening at the same time. Allow students to work for a few minutes, and then switch roles.

Moving Statues *(cont.)*

6. Tell pairs of students to create new moving statues using locomotor movements (movements from place to place). They must move slowly so that their partner can follow along.

7. Have two sets of partners join together in a group of four to form a symmetrically moving statue. Once a moving statue is formed, invite other students to join one at a time, in pairs, or in triads, depending on the current arrangement of the statue and what number will be necessary to maintain its symmetry. Each time such a joining occurs, students must consider how their shape, level, and movement fit with the statue, and the concept of symmetry will be reinforced.

8. Debrief with students using the Questions for Discussion to facilitate their thinking about the process of creating moving statues and about symmetry. Then, have them complete *Mirror Moves* (page 37) so that they can solidify their thinking and you can further assess their learning.

Questions for Discussion

- What different movements did you make? What movements did you observe?
- Would you rather be the leader or the follower? Why?
- What did you find most challenging? Why?
- Where do you see symmetry in the world?
- Why do you think many people find symmetry pleasing?

Moving Statues (cont.)

Specific Grade Level Ideas

K–2

Students can explore the mirroring exercise in order to develop readiness for symmetry. To brainstorm a variety of movements, invite students to close their eyes, if they are comfortable, and slowly move their arms any way they wish while staying in the same place. (For some students, closing their eyes helps them feel comfortable making movements without worrying about what others are doing.) After a minute or so, have students open their eyes and brainstorm. On chart paper, record a list of verbs to describe their movement, such as *raise*, *lower*, *bend*, *point*, *circle*, *swing*, and *stretch*. These words can be used in future movement work to spark ideas. Feel free to suggest ideas yourself. Record the word *axial*, and define it as the name of movements made while you stay in the same place. Reinforce the idea that all of the movements on the list are axial movements.

Double facts (e.g., 3 + 3 = 6) can be explored by having students face each other in even rows. If you have access to a large mirror, students will enjoy moving in a line of four and then turning to look at their reflection in the mirror to see an image of eight as they model 4 + 4 = 8.

Grades 3–5

Students can expand on the explorations in pairs. Have pairs work in different positions. Can they mirror each other as they stand back to back? What about when they stand side by side? Allow time for both students to lead and follow.

Have a few volunteers demonstrate their ability to copy each other's movements. Discuss when the images look symmetrical and when they do not. Note that when students are standing side by side and they both lift their right arms, the total image will be asymmetric. Such an arrangement is fine, but encourage students to note this and talk about how they should move if they wish to maintain reflective symmetry.

Don't be surprised if students continue to talk about symmetry in the days that follow. A few days after the completion of this activity, a fourth-grade student noted, "I was just thinking about shapes. Squares can have diagonal lines of symmetry. People can't."

Moving Statues *(cont.)*

Grades 6–8

Students can use locomotor movements to explore translations and rotational symmetry. Students will need to coordinate their movements carefully to translate (slide) exactly from one location to another. For rotational symmetry, one student can represent the center about which other members of the statue move. Depending on their arrangement, they may want to freeze when a rotational symmetry is formed and then rotate again until the next rotational symmetry is formed. For example, if the statue's base is like that of a regular triangle, the group can rotate 120 degrees three times. The last freeze will be a copy of their original formation, as they would have turned a complete 360 degrees.

Name _____ Date _____

Mirror Moves

Directions: Answer the questions.

1. What words could you use to describe your creative movement?

   _____

   _____

   _____

2. What skills does it take to be a good mirror?

   _____

   _____

   _____

3. What do you have to think about when you join a moving statue trying to maintain symmetry?

   _____

   _____

   _____

4. How would you define *symmetry*?

   _____

   _____

   _____

5. How would you define *asymmetry*?

   _____

   _____

   _____

Experimentation

Model Lesson: Math Discoveries

Model Lesson Overview

Through movement experimentation, students use their bodies as manipulatives to physically discover properties and generalizations related to addition, subtraction, multiplication, and division. This form of physical experimentation is best used when students' ideas exist only at an intuitive level. As they explore these mathematical concepts through movement, they discover aspects of mathematics that they can translate into mathematical symbols.

Standards

K–2
- Adds and subtracts whole numbers
- Uses basic nonlocomotor/axial movements
- Uses locomotor movements in different directions

3–5
- Multiplies and divides whole numbers
- Uses basic nonlocomotor/axial movements
- Uses locomotor movements in different directions

6–8
- Adds, subtracts, multiplies, and divides integers and rational numbers
- Understands the action and movement elements observed in dance, and knows appropriate movement/dance vocabulary

Materials

- *Task Card* (page 44, taskcard.pdf)
- Number line large enough to walk on *(optional)*
- Hundred board large enough to walk on *(optional)*
- *Experiment Summary* (page 45, experimentsummary.pdf)

Experimentation (cont.)

Preparation

This activity as written addresses students' understanding of the commutative property of addition. Other ideas are provided in the Specific Grade Level Ideas. Decide the appropriate focus for your students and model its exploration on this exemplar, developing your own *Task Card* (page 44), if desired.

If you don't have a large number line or hundred board available, you can make the number line on butcher paper and the hundred board on a large plastic tablecloth.

Procedure

1. Invite a group of students to an open area. With students, brainstorm and record a list of movement verbs for students to reference throughout the lesson, such as *wave*, *crumble*, *swing*, *push*, *turn*, and *twist*.

2. Choose one of the movements, such as *twist*, and give students time to explore ways in which they can make twist movements (e.g., twist their whole bodies back and forth, point one foot and twist it back and forth, twist their pinky finger). After some exploration with the movement, ask students to brainstorm as you record different types of twists students could make. Work through several other movements in this same manner, creating a list of possible movements from which students can draw ideas.

3. Group students in pairs. Give each pair a copy of the *Task Card* (page 44). Explain to students that they should pick two movements, one for each student. Provide time for the pairs to explore the movements they would like to use. Then, direct students to create a combination of movements in which the first student performs his or her selected movement five times and then the second student performs his or her movement two times. Remind students that they can draw movement ideas from the list of movements created earlier.

4. Have pairs demonstrate their combination of movements. After each presentation, ask the viewers to name the movements they saw. Have the pairs show their movement combinations again as viewers count aloud to determine the total number of movements (7).

5. Ask, "How would you describe the different movements you saw? What equation could we write to represent the number of creative movements each pair made?" Write the equation for students to see ($5 + 2 = 7$).

Experimentation *(cont.)*

6. Repeat steps 3–5, having students exchange their order so that the second partner makes his or her two movements first and then the other partner follows with five movements. Again, have partners repeat the movements. As viewers, have students count to find the total number of movements. Ask, "What equation could we write to represent these creative movements?" Write the equation $2 + 5 = 7$ under the first equation.

7. Have pairs choose two different numbers and a set of repeated movements, designating each number, such as 5 twists and 3 pulses. One student presents the creative movements, and then the other student represents them in the opposite order. If a large number line or hundred board is available, invite students to make these movements on the line or board, performing one movement on each number before moving to the next. After demonstrating the two different orders, both students should remain at the final number. Ask viewing students to identify the related equations for the movements these two students made, and record them as well.

8. Repeat until students are ready to generalize their discovery about the commutative property in their own words.

9. Debrief with students using the Questions for Discussion. Have students record their thinking in the *Experiment Summary* (page 45).

Questions for Discussion

- What other mathematical examples might we try through movement?

- How might we use words to describe the movement choices?

- How would you describe the mathematical ideas explored in the creative movement?

- How might we use symbols to describe what we see happening?

- Do you think this will happen every time? Why do you think so? Describe your process of translating movement ideas into mathematical equations.

- How would you describe your discovery process?

Experimentation *(cont.)*

Specific Grade Level Ideas

K–2

Kindergarten students can work on combining numbers with sums to 10. Second-grade students and some first-grade students will be able to work with symbolic representation of the commutative property. First- and second-grade students can also explore the inverse relationship between addition and subtraction by creating a series of movements that suggests a doing and undoing. Show students the equation $7 + 3 = 10$ and ask them to use movement to show what else they know (e.g., $3 + 7 = 10$, $10 - 3 = 7$, and $10 - 7 = 3$).

Other potential experiments include exploring the commutative property with greater numbers. Not all students generalize from one-digit examples. Have students look at different ways to creatively combine two numbers of movements for a given total number. Such an experiment could facilitate students' discovery of all the possible combinations of 10.

Work with students to count forward 10 numbers on a hundred board. Allow students to discover that moving across 10 numbers one step at a time gives the same result as moving directly down to the next 10 in one movement. Note they should move creatively within these movements, perhaps choosing slow movement when making a set of 10 consecutive one-step movements and a high-intensity movement, such as leaping when moving down 10 in one movement.

Experimentation *(cont.)*

3–5

Students can explore the activity as written to formalize the commutative property. Remember that students are free to improvise their movement as they explore the mathematical parameters given. Other potential experiments include exploring the associative property of addition: $(x + y) + z = x + (y + z)$. The parameter is that students experiment with the order in which they combine three groups to find their total.

Help students explore patterns among multiples. Have small groups of students choose a number and move in creative ways to show that number's multiples on the hundreds board. One member of the group must be left on each multiple as it is found. A few other students from the audience could then continue the pattern. So if the number 5 is chosen, the first student would move creatively to 5 and stand there, the second to 10, the third to 15, and so forth. After six students are standing on the board, ask questions to stimulate thinking, such as, "What do you think the board will look like if we continue? Why do you think there are two people standing in each row of the chart? How many spaces are there between each person? What connections can we make between how we are standing and the remainders we get when we divide by five?" Common multiples can be explored by students moving according to different numbers and discovering where more than one student lands. So if the students standing on the multiples of 5 remained while the activity is repeated for the multiples of 6, two students will be standing on 30, the first common multiple of 5 and 6.

Experimentation (cont.)

6–8

Have students explore the addition and subtraction of negative and positive numbers. Too often, these processes are taught as a set of rules such as "two negatives make a positive." Have students create a model by moving on a large number line. For example, how might they model 7 – 2? How would this be different from 7 – (–2)? Will they move forward or backward? Will they face the positive or negative end of the line? The goal is for students to create movement explorations, using their growing knowledge of shape, level, and tempo that expand their understanding of how to add and subtract positive and negative numbers.

Students can look at the generalization of the properties of arithmetic. As properties are introduced in the earlier grades with whole numbers, not all students will recognize that they apply to all rational numbers. Furthermore, at this grade level, properties are often listed as abstract rules that have not been developed through concrete models. Have students explore an expression such as –2(4 – 6) and have them physically confirm the distributive property.

Name _____ Date _____

Task Card

Creative Movement Choices:

- The first mover makes 5 movements.

- Then, the second mover makes 2 movements.

You Decide:

- Who will move first and who will move second.

- What creative movements you will make.

- How you will make your movement choices creative and interesting.

Name _____ Date _____

Experiment Summary

Directions: Write your answers in the boxes.

What numbers/operations did you explore in your experiment?	Use movement words to describe your artistic choices.
Make a sketch to show what you observed as you created movement representations of mathematical ideas.	Use math to show what you discovered through movement.

Choreography

Model Lesson: Grouping

Model Lesson Overview

Students plan, or *choreograph*, creative movement, focusing on the location of people (or objects) and the pathways they follow, and represent that plan on paper. They can also consider *tempo*. As students present the movement planned, they gain a kinesthetic experience of the grouping process as well as a visual reminder that numbers are conserved, that is, their rearrangement does not change their value. The focus is on grouping by tens, emphasizing the concept that 10 ones is also 1 ten. This notion permeates our number system and should be explored over time at all levels.

Standards

K–2

- Uses base-ten concepts to compare whole-number relationships and represent them in flexible ways
- Uses locomotor movements in different directions
- Uses movements in straight and curved pathways

3–5

- Understands the basic meaning of place value
- Uses base-ten concepts to represent decimals and fractions in flexible ways
- Uses locomotor movements in different directions
- Uses movements in straight and curved pathways

6–8

- Understands the relationships among equivalent number representations and the advantages and disadvantages of each type of representation
- Memorizes and reproduces movement sequences

Choreography *(cont.)*

Materials

- Snap cubes (*optional*)

- Musical selections

- *Pathways* (page 53, pathways.pdf)

- Bright piece of construction paper

- *Choreography Planner* (pages 54–55, choreographyplanner.pdf)

- *Choreography Map* (page 56, choreographymap.pdf)

Preparation

Think about how students will best work together. To encourage all students to be involved in the problem-solving process, the choreography planning is best completed among 2–4 students. You also need to decide the best way to organize the presentation of the creative movement. One method would be to have the choreographers describe and map their ideas and have ten other classmates enact them. This technique allows students to practice their communication skills and makes the grouping clear. Another approach would be to have the choreographers demonstrate their own creative movement choices using objects, such as snap cubes, a series of movements, or their fingers. Such an approach allows the movement to be presented by the students who know them best and for the grouping of greater numbers.

You will want to use an open meeting area, create an open space in the classroom, or plan to use another open space such as the gym or the cafeteria for the creative-movement presentations. Provide a few musical selections from which students can choose one to use, or provide one recording for all students.

An introductory grouping of 10 ones to 1 ten is described in the Procedure, but it is also easily adapted to other place values. Read the Specific Grade Level Ideas and decide how to best adapt it for your students.

Choreography (cont.)

Procedure

1. Begin by posing the question, "When you see people waiting for a bus or at a park, how might you know which of them are together?" Encourage a variety of responses, such as how close the people are standing together, whether they touch, where their eyes are looking, or how their feet are placed. Invite three or four students to stand and demonstrate how they might look if they were strangers waiting for a bus and how they might look if they were waiting for the bus on their way to see a movie together. Invite another group of students to do the same. Following the demonstrations, have the observers describe the clues that let them know which examples were of people who were in a group together and which were not. Discuss which movements and physical stances suggest relationship.

2. Display the term *pathway* and define it as the path a movement or combination of movements can take. Distribute copies of *Pathways* (page 53) to students, which illustrates five possible paths: *straight*, *zigzag*, *curve*, *spiral*, and *circle*. Have students stand up and explore, making a variety of movements along the different pathways.

3. After students return to their seats, randomly identify ten students to stand in separate locations around the edge of an open space, and place a bright piece of construction paper in the middle. Tell students that when the music starts to play, they are going to move in a specific type of pathway that ends on the marked spot. Call on a volunteer to name a type of pathway to use and start the music.

4. Challenge students to move along these pathways in an interesting way. Ask them to explore all the ways they can move along the path, incorporating movement choices, such as levels (high, medium, low), different tempos (fast vs. slow), and using a variety of ways of moving (hopping, twisting, sliding, etc.). When students are in physical proximity to the marked spot, stop the music and tell them to position themselves to suggest that they are in relationship with each other as one group. Then, restart the music, and have the ten movers leave the group one at a time, following the pathway back to their original positions.

5. Have students discuss what they saw. Ask, "How many students made pathways?" (*10*) "How many groups of 10 did they form?" (*1*) "How do we name this number?" (*10*) "How did the movers show they were one group? What mathematical ideas were represented? What directions would another group need to make these movements?"

Choreography *(cont.)*

6. Explain to students that *choreography* is planning movement sequences. Divide students into small groups. Explain that each group is going to choreograph movement that focuses on grouping by tens and ones. They can choreograph for ten or more people or use objects as their "movers." Their planned movements should be made along specified pathways as groups come together and break apart. They can also consider tempo. (If appropriate, extend the activity to two-digit numbers or different place values. See the Specific Grade Level Ideas.)

7. Give students the *Choreography Planner* (pages 54–55) and have them answer the questions to help them choreograph their movement. Then, have students record the directions for their choreography on the *Choreography Map* (page 56).

8. Have students present their choreographed pieces by having student volunteers follow the directions on the *Choreography Map* (page 56) or by having group members move and manipulate objects to show the choreography. Encourage students to add dramatic moments to their movements by asking, "What emotion might you show when you combine to form a new value? How might your tempo change as you get closer to one another? What might happen if one part doesn't want to be part of the new group?"

9. Use the Questions for Discussion to guide discussion of the presentations.

Questions for Discussion

- What was similar or different about the choreography?

- What did the movers do to let you know they were forming one group?

- How did the group separate into ones?

- What numbers were shown?

- If there was 1 group of ten and 3 ones, what number was shown?

- What movement pathways did you see?

- In what ways did the presentations include interesting moments?

- What struck you about the creative choices that were made in the exploration of movement pathways?

Choreography *(cont.)*

Specific Grade Level Ideas

K–2

Kindergarten students can explore numbers up to 10 without using the reproducibles. Use this strategy to facilitate students' understanding of the teen numbers as 1 ten plus some ones. First- and second-grade students can explore making two-digit numbers as well as a group of 10 tens to form 1 hundred. To begin, ask students representing tens to each raise 10 fingers one by one while moving to a new location and then clasp their hands together to show that there is a complete group of ten. To show a hundred, the 10 students showing tens can come together to make a huddle, perhaps stamping their feet once as they do so. Ask students if they have other ideas for showing the creation of a unit of ten. Try out a range of ideas and discuss them. Ask students how they might use creative movement ideas to show groupings of ten, linking intentional movement, counts, and creative choices to a compelling representation of grouping. Students can draw simple choreography plans on large blank paper by making *X*s to represent the movers and drawing simple pathways.

Pay attention to how students recognize the numbers modeled. For example, if 6 students have raised their 10 fingers, do the observing students count by tens from 10 to 60 or count the tens by ones and recognize the 6 groups of 10 as 60 when asked to identify the number? Are they comfortable counting either way?

Students can also practice shape recognition. Identify a pathway for each shape. Have students choose an object in the room and bring it to a central location, moving according to the shape they found.

Students can work with counting and choreographing movement patterns. For example, ask students to create a movement piece that links a pattern of 5 spirals plus 6 twists plus 10 pulses. They choose what parts of their bodies to move and how to move them, and small groups put the patterns together and present.

Choreography *(cont.)*

3–5

Students can demonstrate more complicated grouping; for example, the thousands can be grouped as 10 hundreds or tenths as ones. Three- or four-digit numbers might be indicated by using different body levels that correspond to the place values (highest thousands, high hundreds, middle tens, low ones). Students can choreograph a sequence of movements in which 10 hundredths become tenths, tenths become ones, ones become tens, tens become hundreds, and so forth. Students could hold a stack of cards that show the different place values (0.01, 0.1, 1, 10...). As the next grouping process begins, movers could identify their new values by putting that number at the front of their stack.

Encourage students to add creative interest to their choreography. For example, one member could be reluctant to join a group or keep trying to escape, or a gatherer could gather blocks to form a tower but keep miscounting so that the tower has to fall down. Remind students that they are not acting out scenes; they are using their bodies to show ideas through creative-movement choices.

Students can also choreograph fractions forming wholes. Have students cut a large rectangle into parts, label each part, and place the parts around the room to be gathered to form a whole. Additional sheets of paper can represent wholes as needed. Or, to emphasize that fractions are numbers, have students collect strips of paper of equal size and two labels, one for zero and one to represent fractions represented on a number line. Simple groupings of fractions with the same denominators can be presented, or unlike denominators and mixed numbers can also be included.

Students' choreography plans can indicate a variety of pathways as well as locations. They can also indicate the order in which the movers (or objects) are joined or removed from a group.

Choreography *(cont.)*

6–8

Students can also explore the ideas provided in the 3–5 Specific Grade Level Ideas. Grouping parts as wholes should focus on mixed numbers, unlike denominators, or combinations of fractions and decimals.

If your classroom has a tile floor, identify an intersecting point of the tiles as the origin (0, 0). Choreographers can then designate locations on their plans by identifying the coordinate points. Each mover can work with multiple pathways in the development of their movement sequence. For example, they could combine straight, zigzag, and curved pathways as they move from one location to another. This requires more detailed notation.

Name _____ Date _____

Pathways

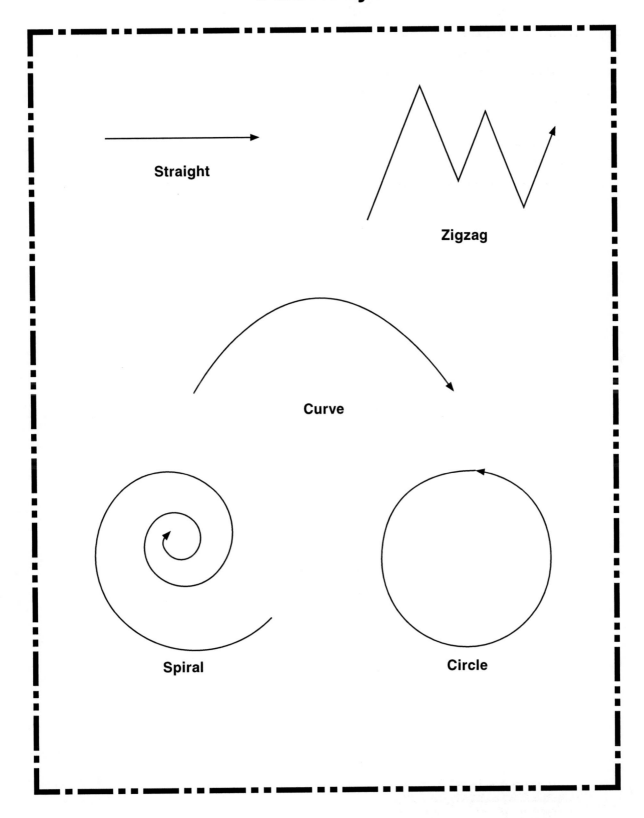

Name _____ Date _____

Choreography Planner

Directions: Answer each question.

1. What number(s) will your choreography show?

   _____

   _____

2. Where will your movers start?

   _____

   _____

   _____

3. What pathways will they follow?

   _____

   _____

   _____

4. What creative movement choices will you ask your movers to use as they move along pathways?

   _____

   _____

   _____

5. How will they move along the pathways?

   _____

   _____

   _____

Choreography Planner *(cont.)*

6. How will the group know when to come together or break apart?

_____

_____

_____

7. Will the group form (or separate) at once or one at a time?

_____

_____

8. How will you show where the group will form?

_____

_____

_____

9. What notes should you add to your plan?

_____

_____

_____

10. How could you add heightened interest to the presentation?

_____

_____

_____

_____

Name _____ Date _____

Choreography Map

Directions: Use the questions to help plan your choreography.

1. Show where the movers (or objects) will be when they are grouped.

2. Show where the movers (or objects) will be when they are not grouped.

3. Use arrows to indicate pathways.

```



```

Write directions for your choreography.

_____

_____

_____

_____

_____

_____

_____

Movement Phrases

Model Lesson: Linking Movement Ideas

Model Lesson Overview

Deep understanding of mathematical concepts requires students to make connections among various ideas. In this strategy, students portray mathematical ideas or processes by linking movements to form movement phrases. For example, students might explore how quadrilaterals can be transformed to represent different types of four-sided polygons or explore examples that lead to generalizations that can be expressed in algebraic equations. Students also focus on the qualities of movement, such as *sustained*, *swing*, *percussive*, *collapse*, as well as vibratory and effort combinations, such as a *float*, *dab*, *punch*, and *glide*, as they develop their movement phrase.

Standards

K–2

- Adds and subtracts whole numbers

- Solves real-world problems involving addition and subtraction of whole numbers

- Creates a dance phrase, repeats it, and varies it

3–5

- Multiplies and divides whole numbers

- Knows approximate size of basic standard units and relationships between them

- Creates a dance phrase, repeats it, and varies it

6–8

- Uses basic and advanced procedures while performing the processes of computation

- Understands choreographic principles, processes, and structures

9–12

- Uses basic and advanced procedures while performing the processes of computation

- Understands choreographic principles, processes, and structures

Materials

- *Six Qualities of Movement Reference Sheet* (pages 62–63, movementreference.pdf)

- *Movement Phrase Graphic Organizer* (page 64, mpgraphicorganizer.pdf)

Movement Phrases *(cont.)*

Preparation

Explore the Specific Grade Level Ideas and decide which mathematical concepts you would like students to investigate through the development of movement phrases. Identify how many students will work together to create a movement phrase. Read the *Six Qualities of Movement Reference Sheet* (pages 62–63) to become familiar with these descriptions of movement.

Procedure

1. Ask students how they link ideas in their writing. Talk about the importance of giving examples and connecting ideas. Explain to students that when we connect movements, we create movement phrases and that such sequences can describe and represent the essence of a mathematical idea.

2. Introduce the mathematical concept that you have chosen, and assign groups. Give students a few minutes to talk in their groups about different components of the idea, the sequence of different steps in the mathematics procedure, and the important mathematical ideas associated with each component or step. Have groups share their thinking with the class. Record responses for students to refer to throughout the lesson, and encourage them to also take notes.

3. Ask students to talk in small groups about how they could represent these ideas by exploring and conveying ideas in a compelling way through creative movement. Have groups share their thinking and again record their ideas as students also take notes. Students will generate a list of movement choices that they can weave together in a sequence to create their movement phrase.

4. Display or distribute the *Six Qualities of Movement Reference Sheet* (pages 62–63) and review the ideas with students. Note that the goal is not to have students memorize this list but to offer students new ways to think about how a movement is executed and thus communicated in nuanced ways. Allow time for students to investigate some of the movements they have identified in their discussion, applying different movement qualities to them. For example, how might they turn their heads in a sustained manner rather than in a swinging, pendular one? Have students explore different combinations of movements and qualities and take notes about those that they found worked well together.

5. Distribute the *Movement Phrase Graphic Organizer* (page 64) and explain to students that they will use it to summarize their thinking. Have students work in their groups to identify at least three components or steps they will represent in their movement phrase along with the mathematical ideas, movements, and movement qualities to be used.

Movement Phrases *(cont.)*

6. Encourage students to explore different combinations of movements before they make final choices. Use the Planning Questions to guide their thinking. Their decisions should be recorded in the *Movement Phrase Graphic Organizer*.

7. Ask students to discuss and then indicate the sequence of the components in their movement phrases by numbering them on the organizer.

8. Tell students to identify how they will use creative movement to transition from one component to the next. Students should record these decisions in the links between the components.

9. Give students time to explore their choices physically and to rehearse their phrase until they are ready to present it to the larger group.

10. Have groups present their pieces. Ask students to begin and end in stillness in order to heighten the experience for the other groups.

11. Ask the viewers to observe the movement presentations closely and to identify the ideas being portrayed. Use the Questions for Discussion to prompt students' reflections on their process of translating ideas into movement and on what viewers saw in the movement phrase that suggested the mathematical idea.

Planning Questions

- How might we show this idea through movement?

- How will your creative movement choices communicate the mathematical ideas?

- What might this look like as ideas are linked together in a sequence?

- How might we connect these ideas together in smooth transitions so that one math movement idea flows into the next?

- How does your movement sequence communicate like a sentence?

Questions for Discussion

- How did you break the mathematical ideas down into movement parts?

- What movement choices did you make to highlight mathematical ideas?

- How did your movement phrase work to reveal the mathematical ideas?

- How did mathematical ideas inform the development of your movement phrase?

- As you were observing the work of others, what struck you about the movement?

- As you were observing the work of others, what struck you about the math?

Movement Phrases (cont.)

Specific Grade Level Ideas

K–2

Work with students in small groups. Students can demonstrate basic fact strategies along a number line to change, for example, 9 + 4 to 10 + 3 or 9 + 1 + 3, or 12 − 7 to 12 − 2 − 5. First, have students discuss their fact strategies and then talk about movements that would exemplify them.

3–5

Students can follow the procedure as written. Take time to review the terms on the *Six Qualities of Movement Reference Sheet* to increase students' confidence with the vocabulary.

Ideas to explore include the steps within strategies for multi-digit addition, subtraction, multiplication, or division, such as changing numbers to form a friendlier example and then compensating for the change, and the relationships among units of measure for time, length, or capacity.

Movement Phrases *(cont.)*

6–8

Students can follow the procedure as written. Students' exploration can include proportional reasoning where they show a physical model that is shrunk and then enlarged to determine if two store items have the same unit price.

Have students work on techniques for solving equations; such a movement phrase does not need to be a literal representation of the calculating but rather representational of the characteristic approaches employed such as doing something to both sides of an equation in order to maintain equality or using substitution.

Students could show models when x has a value of 1 and 2 and 3. The linked representations should allow viewers to identify the slope and y-intercept and thus the equation depicted.

Students can list the computational steps in the order of operations, use the standard algorithm for division, find the mean average, make their own graphic organizers to use once they have identified the steps, create movements to represent each step, and then link their representations to illustrate the order within the procedures.

9–12

Students can create movement phrases to represent the process of completing the square, using systems of equations, or informally proving how to find the volume of a cone, a cylinder, or a pyramid. For example, students could create a movement phrase that shows how they would first focus on the middle term of a trinomial and then square half of that number to complete the square. Or students could create a phrase that illustrates the 1:3 relationship between the area of a pyramid and rectangular prism with the same height and base.

Six Qualities of Movement Reference Sheet

Percussive:

Percussive movements are quick, forceful, and sudden. They are broken up by quick pauses. Think of someone suddenly stomping his or her feet and pausing briefly afterward to increase the impact of the movement.

Sustained:

Sustained movements are flowing, ongoing, and smooth. Think of sliding your foot out away from your body in a long, fluid push.

Vibratory:

Vibratory movements are similar to percussive ones, but they are quicker and less forceful. The movements could involve tapping or shaking.

Six Qualities of Movement
Reference Sheet *(cont.)*

Suspension:

A suspension movement is the slight pause that occurs between motions. The pause can draw attention to the movement just before or after.

Collapse:

Collapse movements give in to the pull of gravity. They can be sudden movements, such as a quick fall to the floor, or they can be gradual motions, such as the controlled lowering of your leg.

Swing/Pendular:

A swing or pendular movement goes back and forth. An example would be an arm that swings up high, pauses briefly, and then returns back down.

Name _____ Date _____

Movement Phrase Graphic Organizer

Directions: Fill in the charts.

Idea #1 _____

Math Ideas:	
Movements	Qualities

Idea #2 _____

Math Ideas:	
Movements	Qualities

Idea #3 _____

Math Ideas:	
Movements	Qualities

Drama

Drama

Understanding Drama

Students don't always see an immediate connection between mathematical concepts and their lives or interests. Drama can provide engaging contexts for exploring mathematical ideas. By enacting scenes that connect to a mathematical concept or skill, students can apply their learning in real-world settings.

When we integrate drama into the mathematics classroom, we invite our students to consider particular situations in which mathematical ideas are embedded. As students explore these scenarios, they uncover and deepen their mathematical thinking, make personal connections to mathematics, and recognize its real-world relevance. Christopher Andersen (2004) notes that drama has the ability to recreate the essential elements in the world; as such, drama can place mathematics in authentic situations that make sense to students.

When students can explore mathematics through the lens of a character, they are called upon to imagine themselves working through processes, events, and dilemmas. In their roles, they must make choices, solve problems, translate concepts, and articulate ideas. This process requires students to explain, persuade, clarify, and negotiate their thinking (Elliott-Johns et al. 2012). As students investigate perspectives that are different from their own, they expand their worldviews and develop an awareness of their own. Such experiences help students clarify their thinking, understand different perspectives, and consider new strategies for solving problems.

Drama will provide your students with contexts in which they can ground their mathematical investigations. And of course, through dramatic explorations, students learn about and develop skills in drama as well.

These drama strategies provide a rich context for mathematical investigations in which students imagine themselves in a variety of math-related situations. Embedding mathematical ideas into dramatic scenarios creates motivation for students to participate eagerly in the exploration of ideas from multiple perspectives.

Drama *(cont.)*

Strategies for Drama

❧ Mantle of the Expert

Developed by dramatist Dorothy Heathcote, this strategy asks students to imagine that they have a particular expertise that informs how they approach the work and how they present their ideas. Inviting students to imagine that they have a specific frame of reference can be a catalyst that deepens their interest and sense of authority in an area of study. Heathcote and Bolton (1995) note, "Thinking from within a situation immediately forces a different kind of thinking. Research has convincingly shown that the determining factor in children's ability to perform particular intellectual tasks is the context in which the task is embedded. In Mantle of the Expert, problems and challenges arise within a context that makes them both motivating and comprehensible."

When students are in a dramatic role, they begin to think through the lens of the character they are playing, consequently developing the attitude and ways of thinking of a mathematical expert. Being asked questions about the decisions they make in their roles, called *hot-seating*, can draw evidence of students' mathematical thinking.

❧ Teacher-in-Role

In process drama, the teacher and students work together to explore a problem or situation in an unscripted manner through improvisation (O'Neill 1995). In this strategy, the teacher takes on the role of a character to introduce a drama. Teachers can model the kind of work that they will ask students to do or set the stage for a dramatic scene. Either way, the strategy serves as an invitation for students to join in the dramatic work, to imagine, or to consider *what if?* There are a variety of ways that the teacher can create this role. For example, the teacher can portray a character in a book who presents his or her perspectives, become a historical character who shares thoughts at a time when a key choice must be made that will have a significant impact on events, or introduce an investigation by depicting a character who shares the details of a scenario and asks others to participate as related characters. The allure of seeing their teacher be willing to engage in the creation of a scene compels students to suspend their disbelief and join in the dramatic enactment.

Drama *(cont.)*

ɞ Tableaux

Tableau is a French word meaning "frozen picture." It is a drama technique that allows for the exploration of an idea without movement or speaking. In this technique, students use their bodies to create a shape or full picture to tell a story, literally represent a concept, or create a tangible representation of an abstract concept. Working with physical stance (low, medium, high), suggested relationships (body placement and eye contact), and a sense of action frozen in time allows students to explore ideas and provides a range of ways for students to share what they know about a concept. One student can create a frozen image, or a group can work together to create an image. The process of creating group tableaux prompts discussion of the characteristics of what is being portrayed. The learning process occurs in the translation of ideas to physical representation.

ɞ Enacting Scenes

The bread and butter of drama is the development and enactment of scenes. Students portray characters that find themselves in particular settings and influenced by specific circumstances. They make choices, solve problems, and react to relationships with other characters. We watch (or participate ourselves) as characters play out choices and deal with implications as the drama unfolds. Scenes are valuable thinking frames and can be used flexibly across content and contexts. Students can enter a scene suggested by someone else or create their own in response to mathematical problems. Drama allows abstract ideas to become concrete and enjoyable, and it increases the pace at which children learn mathematical ideas (Erdoğan and Baran 2009).

ɞ Monologue

A *monologue* is a dramatic scene performed by one person. In creating a monologue, students take the perspective of a character in a story, real or imagined, and speak directly to the audience for one to three minutes. The character must be established without interactions with others (that would be a dialogue) and must speak in a way that engages the audience with this singular focus.

There are often monologues in stories and plays that illuminate what a character is thinking. Most often, a monologue reveals a conflict of some kind that the character is wrestling with, perhaps a choice to be made or a problem to be solved. Note that variations include *soliloquy* in which a character is speaking to him-or herself. The creation of a monologue provides the opportunity to investigate what Barry Lane calls a "thoughtshot" of a character's inner thinking (1992).

Drama (cont.)

∞ Monologue (cont.)

This strategy allows students to "get into the head" of a particular character. Eventually, the goal is for students to create their own monologues, but you may want to introduce the strategy by having students explore prepared monologues in resources such as *Magnificent Monologues for Kids 2* by Chambers Stevens and *Minute Monologues for Kids* by Ruth Mae Roddy. Then, students can develop characters and create and perform monologues for inanimate objects or forces, or they can portray specific characters (a historical figure, a character from a book, a newspaper article, or a painting), or they can create an imagined character. In order for a monologue to be dramatic, the character must have some tension or conflict that he or she is wrestling with. This conflict can be an internal or external dilemma. Its resolution or the naming of it will create dramatic interest.

Mantle of the Expert

Model Lesson: Designing Math Exhibits

Model Lesson Overview

In this strategy, students are asked to take on the expert role of a museum exhibit designer, present their ideas in role, and answer questions about their exhibit. The experts are charged with engaging young people in interactive math. This flips students' usual roles, and they suddenly find that *they* are educators and must consider how to bring math to life for young people. Students watching the presentations will imagine that they are administrators meeting with museum educators to hear their ideas and probe each group's vision further with questions.

Standards

K–2

- Counts whole numbers

- Knows processes for telling time, counting money, and measuring length, weight, and temperature, using basic standard and non-standard units

- Knows how to interact in improvisations

3–5

- Multiplies and divides whole numbers

- Selects and uses appropriate units of measurement, according to type and size of unit

- Knows how to interact in improvisations

6–8

- Understands the basic concepts of center and dispersion of data

- Organizes and displays data using tables, graphs, frequency distributions, and plots

- Interacts as an invented character in improvised and scripted scenes

9–12

- Uses a variety of models to represent functions, patterns, and relationships

- Develops, communicates, and sustains characters that communicate with audiences in improvisations and informal or formal productions

Materials

- *Sample Museum Director Memo* (page 75, directormemo.pdf)

- *Brainstorming Guide* (page 76, brainstormingguide.pdf)

Mantle of the Expert *(cont.)*

Preparation

Identify the exhibit theme you would like the groups to work on. Possible themes are offered in the Specific Grade Level Ideas. Read the *Sample Museum Director Memo* (page 75) and decide how to adapt it for your students. If time allows, visit museum exhibits in person or online.

Procedure

1. Invite students to imagine that they work at a museum in the education department. Their role consists of planning and designing new educational exhibits for young people. Tell students that they will receive a memo from the director of the museum with their next installation-design assignment. Use the *Sample Museum Director Memo* (page 75) as is, or customize it for your students. Tell them that they will improvise, or create in the moment, as they imagine that they are actually exhibit designers and act accordingly.

2. Divide students into small groups of three or four so groups can work together to brainstorm and plan their exhibits. Then, distribute the *Sample Museum Director Memo* to each group. Have students read the memo in groups and discuss the idea they have been assigned. Each group should receive the same concept, which will serve to show how the mathematical idea can be approached from many perspectives. Sharing the same focus also deepens the knowledge of the group in a particular area so that when students are watching other presentations, they will be able to ask in-depth questions about the presentations.

3. Distribute the *Brainstorming Guide* (page 76) and have students work together to complete it. Check in with groups as they are working to hear their preliminary ideas, to help form their design concepts for the exhibit, and to prompt them to consider how to present their design ideas. Use the Planning Questions to guide students' thinking. Resource materials can be gathered and shared.

4. Once groups have completed the *Brainstorming Guide*, tell them to plan their presentation and then rehearse it. Watch each group rehearse and provide feedback. Tell students that as each group presents, students who are not involved in the presentation will act as the panel of administrators who will be making the selection of what will be included in the exhibit. Then, invite the exhibit designers to present their ideas to the panel. Note that following each presentation, members of the panel will ask questions so that they can make informed decisions about the exhibit.

Mantle of the Expert *(cont.)*

5. Direct each group to introduce the characters in their team and present their ideas in a dramatic presentation. During the presentations, the administrative panel should note questions to ask during a question-and-answer period following the presentation.

6. Facilitate a final conversation in which the exhibit designers and administrators note the features of the presentations that were most effective in presenting math in a compelling way. This work could be further developed into real exhibits that are presented to other classes.

Planning Questions

- What do you already know about this math concept?

- What do you need to know?

- What evidence can you show of problem-solving strategies?

- How can you explain computational strategies?

- What examples can you come up with from the real world?

- How can you explain the ways in which your exhibit will engage young people?

- How can you use your expertise as an education exhibit designer to convince administrators that this design deserves to be created?

- How will you present your ideas showing how the exhibit will engage young people?

Specific Grade Level Ideas

K–2

Ask the education exhibit designers to create a plan for an exhibit that shows math on the playground. As part of their exhibit plan, invite students to sketch a map of their school playground with details, including, for example, the heights of different equipment, the numbers of steps on specific structures, the height between treads on a climbing wall, and/or what shapes are embedded in the playground equipment. Ask students to note math in techniques for deciding who goes first, such as one potato, two potato; even and odd; and so forth. As a challenge, students can create and present imaginary playgrounds or add specific features to enhance existing structures.

Mantle of the Expert *(cont.)*

3–5

Ask the education exhibit designers to create an exhibit that features party planning and math. As museum visitors engage with the exhibit, they can create the full menu for the event and figure out how much to order based on guest attendance and how many people each food item will serve (pizza slices, drinks per gallon, etc.). Students can also calculate the cost of each item and how much the overall party will cost.

6–8

Education exhibit designers can explore the idea as presented in the *Sample Museum Director Memo*. Designers also can consider statistics in a variety of areas, such as data related to the use of social media.

9–12

Ask students to design an exhibit related to mathematical modeling. Provide a real-world example, such as the growth of bacteria. Then, have students create related exhibits by choosing themes such as environmental disasters, health epidemics, or "going viral" on the Internet.

Name _____   Date _____

Sample Museum Director Memo

To: Museum Education Exhibit Design Team
From: Museum Director
Re: Math Installation-Design Assignment

As you know, we have opened a new wing in the museum that will house an exhibit called *Math Worlds*. We are seeking to develop several ideas about what this exhibit might include and how this exhibit will capture the excitement of math in the world in a way that is engaging for students in your grade.

Your team has a history of creating exemplary exhibit designs. We are inviting you to present your ideas to engage young people in math to our administrative panel. Your exhibit should focus on how sports statistics are calculated (batting averages, comparative averages, etc.). Please find time to meet with your team, research this area, and develop good examples of what might be included in your exhibit.

You will present your findings to the administrative panel in three weeks. Please be prepared not only to make a compelling case for your proposed exhibit and how it will engage young learners, but also to answer questions from the administrative panel. Good luck, and I look forward to hearing your creative math ideas.

Name _____ Date _____

Brainstorming Guide

Directions: Fill in the chart to organize your ideas for your museum exhibit. Attach sketches of potential layouts for your exhibit.

Math Concept:	
Real-Life Example:	
Initial Ideas for Exhibit:	

Questions to Consider	Ideas
How will this idea be made engaging for the age group attending?	
How will you explain and represent the mathematical ideas?	
How will the exhibit interact with visitors?	

Teacher-in-Role

Model Lesson: The Math Detective

Model Lesson Overview

In this strategy, the teacher invites students to imagine that they are detectives who are skilled in identifying fractions. The teacher begins the scenario by acting as if he or she is a detective who is searching for "Real Math." The detectives, or the students, are convened for a meeting. Identifying places where fractions exist in life gives students a sense of why it's important to understand the math concepts they are learning. The exchange of ideas and sorting of evidence common to detective work allows misconceptions to be addressed. Though this exemplar focuses on detectives, you may vary your role as a detective to other careers that support a variety of content.

Standards

K–2

- Understands the concept of a unit and its subdivision into equal parts

- Understands the visual, aural, oral, and kinetic elements of dramatic performances

3–5

- Understands the concepts related to fractions and decimals

- Understands the visual, aural, oral, and kinetic elements of dramatic performances

6–8

- Understands the concepts of ratio, proportion, and percent and the relationships among them

- Articulates the meanings constructed from one's own and others' dramatic performances

Materials

- *Detective Script* (page 81, detectivescript.pdf)

- Detective props (detective hat, magnifying glass, notepad) (*optional*)

- Evidence-collection tools (tweezers)

- Examples of fractions (a checkerboard, a marked measuring cup, and a clock showing half-past the hour)

- Box to hold items

- Cameras (*optional*)

- *Evidence Chart* (page 82, evidencechart.pdf)

Teacher-in-Role *(cont.)*

Preparation

Review the *Detective Script* (page 81) so that you are comfortable in the role. Adapt the script as needed for your students and area of focus. Feel free to use your own script if you prefer; just make sure your manner of speaking is quite different than usual in order to create a sense of character. You can make the activity more engaging by using a few props, such as a detective hat, magnifying glass, detective notepad, and evidence-collection tools, such as tweezers. Your willingness to be dramatic will intrigue students and help them feel comfortable in taking their own dramatic risks.

Gather examples of fractions, such as a checkerboard, a marked measuring cup, and a picture of the clock showing half-past the hour, and place them in a box to share with students later. Other ideas are provided in the Specific Grade Level Ideas.

Procedure

1. Tell students that you are going to begin a drama that invites them into an investigation of real-world math. They will be asked to join the investigation squad and collect and present their findings as detectives. They will have 24 hours for the search. The idea is to have fun while bringing forward examples of math in their lives. If desired, have students dress the part of a detective when presenting their "evidence" the next day and work with a partner.

2. Excuse yourself from the classroom for a moment, and put on your detective outfit, if desired. Tell students that the scene begins when you say "Curtain up" and ends when you say "Curtain down." Say "Curtain up" when you re-enter the classroom in your detective attire, letting students know that the drama is about to begin.

3. Begin the drama by clearly moving into the detective role as you introduce yourself. Present the challenge to students using the *Detective Script* (page 81).

4. End the drama by telling students that their teacher is returning, but you'll be back tomorrow at the same time to see what they've collected. Say "Curtain down," and leave the room to alert students the drama is ending.

5. Provide time for students to collect evidence of fractions they find in the classroom. Tweezers can be used to handle the evidence with care. Then, extend the activity throughout the day by having students find fractions in other parts of the school and at home.

Teacher-in-Role *(cont.)*

6. Once all evidence is collected, gather students together again to consider their findings. Return to role, and invite students to present their evidence. As students present, have other students use the *Evidence Chart* (page 82) to record additional evidence and continue to probe and ask questions. Invite other detectives to weigh in on the discussion of evidence, developing the collective knowledge of the class. Continue to add words, phrases, and significant ideas to an "evidence wall." Encourage students to report in the role of experts. They are to use their evidence to convince you and their peers of their ideas.

7. Extend students' thinking by continuing the conversation in role, using the Questions for Discussion. Note that they are also asked in role.

Questions for Discussion

- I have heard that fractions can be on a number line. Has anyone found evidence of this?

- Could you help me identify the greatest fraction you found?

- It's been said that the parts of a whole can have different areas. What can we say to stop this rumor?

- I am impressed by your abilities as detectives. Can you explain how you were effective in finding so many examples of fractions?

Specific Grade Level Ideas

K–2

Review the meaning of the word *expert* prior to this activity. Then, give students the opportunity to identify some ways that they are experts. As one first-grade student suggested, "In my family, I am the expert at making my baby sister laugh." The master detective can be a puppet that visits regularly during the course of the year, looking for examples of mathematical concepts being studied at that time.

Other evidence that students can find includes objects that help you to know the length of an inch or a foot, examples of specific shapes, or different strategies used to add or subtract.

Teacher-in-Role *(cont.)*

3–5

Discuss the role of experts prior to the activity. Ask students what they know about experts and how experts can be identified. Have students identify specific ways they recognize experts so that they can call upon these ideas when asked to portray an expert.

Other evidence that students can find includes objects that help you to know mass or liquid measures, properties of specific shapes, or different strategies used to multiply or divide.

6–8

Students can collect mathematical evidence within newspapers and store flyers involving rates, ratios, and percentages, particularly large or small numbers or articles that depend on proportional reasoning. They can also present their own detective role-play to younger students.

Detective Script

Curtain up.

Detective peers around the corner suspiciously.

Good! You have arrived. Mr(s). (insert teacher's name) told me you would be here and ready to help me with my...er...yes, my search. I need your help.

You see, I'm a detective. Who knows what a detective is? I've been asked to find *(looks over shoulder as if checking to make sure no one is listening)* fractions! That's right. Fractions. I'm not entirely sure if I know exactly what they are, but never fear! Detectives detect!

I'm hoping—I mean really hoping—that you'll join me as detectives in training. You will learn that it takes great observation and focus to be a detective. You never know what you'll be asked to find. People, things, evidence of all kinds....

(Looks around the room carefully) Perhaps you know what fractions are. I need your help. I need it desperately. You see, I have...um...one tiny problem. It's the thing I never quite learned in school. And so, I really don't know what to look for! Will you help? Are you in?

I need to know just what a fraction is and how I'll recognize it. Can you help? Just to make sure we're on the same page, let's list the characteristics of the ....er....math evidence we'll need.

Discussion ensues as the detective works with students to give a few examples of where they may find fractions. As the "detectives" make relevant points, sharing their knowledge about concepts and examples, the detective takes notes on the board. These words and phrases can be referred to when they return together with evidence of fractions in hand.

Great! I thank you! I now know what I'm looking for. I think I have a few examples in my bag that fit the description of the evidence you've described. Let's see....

At this point, the detective can share examples with students to solidify their understanding of what they're looking for and how they might record their findings using the Evidence Chart *(page 82).*

Your job, should you choose to accept it, is to locate and document fractions where they occur! You can work with partners. We'll meet in the morning to share what we've found.

But shhhh! Your teacher is coming back—can we keep my...issue...a secret? Thanks. See you tomorrow. Oh, and good luck.

Curtain down.

Name _____ Date _____

Evidence Chart

Directions: Fill in the chart as you collect evidence.

Math Content:	
Description of Evidence	**Description of Math Concepts**

Tableaux

Model Lesson: Math Statues

Model Lesson Overview

In this strategy, students use their bodies to create a tangible representation of an abstract concept. Working with level (low, medium, high), suggested relationships (body placement and eye contact), and a sense of action frozen in time allows students to explore ideas and provides a range of ways for them to share what they know about a concept. Students create *tableaux*, or statues, to represent mathematical ideas and then view the various tableaux created by others, trying to identify the concepts depicted.

Standards

K–2

- Understands basic properties of simple geometric shapes and similarities and differences between simple geometric shapes

- Knows various ways of staging classroom dramatizations

3–5

- Understands basic properties of figures

- Understands characteristics of lines

- Knows various ways of staging classroom dramatizations

6–8

- Understands special values of patterns, relationships, and functions

- Plans visual and aural elements for improvised and scripted scenes

9–12

- Understands and applies basic and advanced concepts of statistics and data analysis

- Communicates directorial choices for improvised or scripted scenes

Materials

- *Gallery Walk Observation Sheet* (page 88, gallerywalk.pdf)

Tableaux (cont.)

Preparation

As you prepare to use this strategy to explore mathematical concepts, think about how to group students so that more complex ideas can be represented. Students can be asked to create a single statue or work in small groups to create larger statues. More complex ideas might be best portrayed in larger groups of five or six. You can ask one student in the group to act as the "sculptor" by guiding the creation of the tableau. Select concepts and identify group size before beginning.

As this activity involves physical interaction, review with students respectful ways to work together if necessary. For example, you might note, "Show your 'clay' how you want them to be positioned by demonstrating it yourself or describing it in words." Other ideas are provided in the Specific Grade Level Ideas.

Procedure

1. Introduce what a *tableau* is by inviting two students to join you. Dramatize being a sculptor as you "mold" their bodies into a triangle. You could, for example, invite one student to stand straight to form one side of the triangle and the other student to bend at the waist and form the other two sides with outstretched arms. Ask the viewers to identify the term dramatized.

2. Repeat, but this time, invite five students to join you and suggest that they arrange themselves to form a variety of triangles. For example, one student could place his or her hands on his or her hips while another bends a leg so that it forms a triangle with the other leg. Have students talk about the differences between making a single sculpture and a group sculpture, and the experience of having a sculptor role and using group decision making.

3. Give students a mathematical term to dramatize through tableaux or ask them to identify one themselves. Then, describe how students will create the tableaux. For example:

   - Have students work in pairs. One student is the "sculptor" and the other is "clay." The sculptor molds the clay into a human sculpture representing a geometric term, such as the name of a shape.

   - Have students work in small groups. One or two group members go to the center of the room and begin the sculpture with a pose. The rest of the participants add on, one by one, to create a group sculpture until all group members are involved. Suggested terms to explore include *perpendicular*, *equal*, and *symmetry*.

Tableaux *(cont.)*

- For more complex ideas, have students create a "slide show" in which they dramatize multiple tableaux that show a progression. Images are presented one right after the other. The viewers can share their thinking about what they have seen following each slide show. The presenters can say "Curtain down" and "Curtain up" between images, indicating that the viewers should close their eyes in between slides so that they see only the still images and not the movement between images.

4. Once students have developed their ideas, have them present their tableaux to the class. You might introduce this by saying, "Imagine we are in an art gallery. We'll walk around and look at the sculptures. At each stop on our gallery walk, we'll talk about what we see, brainstorm what terms you think are being portrayed, and discuss how the tableau suggests the term." Distribute the *Gallery Walk Observation Sheet* (page 88) and tell students, "We'll use this to track the list of the words you use to describe what you see, and we'll find out from our sculptors what the term is and how our guesses relate to the concept represented in the tableau."

5. Depending on the way the tableaux have developed, sculptors could demonstrate their molding of the clay or students could just get into formation. Be sure to provide time for students to review the tableaux. Use the Questions for Discussion to guide students' thinking.

6. As you move around the gallery, have students continue listing words to describe the tableaux. You may want to keep a record as well. You will end up with a rich list of adjectives, synonyms, and metaphors that will allow students to see the mathematical concepts in new ways. Add to the list as each group describes their process of creating tableaux. This is often where ideas are translated and realizations occur. Capturing students' language will reveal the connections they have made.

Questions for Discussion

For the viewers:

- What concept do you think is being represented?

- What words come to mind as you view the sculpture?

- What do you see in the sculpture that suggests the mathematical idea?

- What action is suggested?

- How does this information inform your interpretation of the sculpture?

- What similarities were there in the different sculptures of the same ideas?

- What differences were there in the different sculptures of the same ideas?

Tableaux (cont.)

For the participants in the tableau:

- How did you meet your goal(s)?

- What was the sculpting experience like for you?

- Which ideas were easy to illustrate? Which concepts were more challenging?

- What was it like to join the tableau?

- How did the descriptions offered by the viewers of the tableau match your ideas of the concept being presented?

Specific Grade Level Ideas

K–2

Provide students with vocabulary or concepts that are concrete and easy to enact. Have students use their bodies to create geometric shapes, such as *triangles* or *rectangles*, providing them with the opportunity to embody the idea and develop the skills to hold a shape still. Non-geometric ideas to explore include comparative phrases such as *greater than*, *less than*, *longer than*, or *shorter than*.

3–5

Provide students with the names of geometric shapes, types of angles (*acute*, *obtuse*, or *right*), or *parallel* and *perpendicular* lines to enact. You can also challenge students to enact a term such as *polygon* that will require them to portray a general category and recognize the underlying connection among several examples. Other ideas include *array*, *area*, or *perimeter*. Non-geometric concepts to explore include *remainder*, *fraction*, *equal*, *commutative*, and *associative*.

6–8

Ask students to select a concept from a list of mathematical concepts being explored. When working with particularly abstract ideas such as *functions, proportionality*, *variability*, or *independent variables*, have individual students or pairs of students make a tableau for the same term and then see if the other students can identify the concept from the examples.

Tableaux *(cont.)*

9–12

Assign or have students choose terms or concepts related to a unit on statistics and data analysis. Possible terms include *inverse*, *box plot*, *random*, *distribution*, *correlation*, *compound event*, and *margin of error*.

Name _____   Date _____

Gallery Walk Observation Sheet

Directions: As you observe the tableaux, record your observations in the chart below.

Observation Notes	Tableau 1	Tableau 2	Tableau 3
Words to describe the tableau			
Notes from the sculptor and "clay" about the process			
Concept that is being represented			
What we've learned about the concept			

Enacting Scenes

Model Lesson: Mental Math Commercials

Model Lesson Overview

In this strategy, students imagine that they work for an advertising agency and have been invited to create a commercial for a new "Got Math?" campaign. Each advertisement will include a scene in which a math concept is applied within a real-world context. For the audience (the rest of the class in this case), the scenarios present math problems in engaging ways that trigger interest and curiosity. All students are invited to solve the problems alongside the characters. As a result, students begin to understand why flexible computation and estimation skills are important and are required for everyday life.

Standards

K–2
- Solves real-world problems involving addition and subtraction of whole numbers
- Knows how to interact in improvisations

3–5
- Solves word problems and real-world problems involving number operations
- Knows how to interact in improvisations

6–8
- Selects and uses appropriate computational methods for a given situation
- Interacts as an invented character in improvised and scripted scenes

Materials
- *Scenario Cards* (pages 93–95, scenariocards.pdf)
- Poster board
- Props for scenes *(optional)*

Preparation

Read the scenarios provided in the *Scenario Cards* (pages 93–95) and decide on the tasks appropriate for your students, or provide your own tasks relevant to a current curricular unit. Gather props that will allow students to create rich characters and identify a scene in which mental math would be a natural occurrence such as making purchases, planning a schedule, or keeping records. Other ideas are provided in the Specific Grade Level Ideas.

Enacting Scenes *(cont.)*

Procedure

1. Ask students to help you dramatize a model scene. For example, a middle school scenario could include two women shopping in a dress shop. They come across an amazing gown that costs $230. The gown is on the 30%-off rack with a sign that says, "Today Only! Take Another 20% Off!" The characters have an animated conversation about what a steal this offer provides, and they work to figure out if they have enough money with just $100 in cash in their wallets. Will they leave with or without the dress? Students can create a final caption for their scene such as, "Savvy customers shop for sales. I've saved over $100 in the last two weeks by using mental math in the moment." Have younger students dramatize sharing food items equally at snack time or purchasing simple items.

2. Distribute the *Scenario Cards* (pages 93–95) to students and provide time for students to work in small groups to create the characters and details of the scenarios they will perform. Use the Planning Questions to guide students' thinking.

3. Have students make two posters to hold up during their performance, one that says "Got Math?" and one that says "You Need to Know Your Math!" Have students practice performing their scenes, identifying when math calculations are needed. At this point, they should freeze the scene, hold up their "Got Math?" sign, and allow time for the viewers to figure along with them. They should signal the end of their scene by holding up their "You Need to Know Your Math!" sign.

4. Have students present their scenes to the rest of the class, stopping as planned and holding up their "Got Math?" sign to indicate that they need to calculate the math problem presented. Record the solution strategies as they are suggested for students to refer to throughout the lesson. Once several different strategies are recorded, have students continue the scene. The characters should then calculate the math, and the scene moves on to a natural conclusion. The actors should display the "You Need to Know Your Math!" sign to end the scene. Note that scenes may end up with comedic moments, which add to students' enjoyment of the activity.

5. Debrief the scene using the Questions for Discussion. Highlight how mathematics contributed to the resolution of the characters' situation and return to the list of suggested strategies. Have students compare the strategies according to their mathematical similarities, differences, and ease of use.

Enacting Scenes *(cont.)*

Planning Questions

- How might your math problem unfold in a real-life situation?

- What characters might find themselves in this situation? When?

- What props might you use to help dramatize the need for mathematical information?

- What representations might you make to explain the mathematical thinking that is needed?

- Is there a different mathematical strategy you could use?

- What dramatic strategies might you employ to make the scene feel real?

Questions for Discussion

- Did the audience calculate the answer in the same way that the characters did?

- How else might this calculation be performed?

- In what situations do you find mental math helpful?

- What math skills do you use when you calculate mentally?

- For you, what makes a particular technique easier or more challenging?

- How did the dramatization help in providing an engaging story?

Specific Grade Level Ideas

K–2

Have students think about what they know about counting, time, and money, and how they use this knowledge in their lives. Once example ideas are explored, students can work on creating characters that can demonstrate the use of math in dramatized scenes. Use actual objects (coins, blocks, toys, etc.) as props to make the concepts concrete for students. See the *Scenario Cards* for grades K–2 specific scenarios.

Enacting Scenes *(cont.)*

3–5

If you want students to create their own scenarios, provide them with grocery store flyers or menus to trigger ideas. Allowing students to create characters for each scene with interesting props and costume pieces will increase their investment in the activity. See the *Scenario Cards* for grades 3–5 specific scenarios.

6–8

If you want students to create their own scenarios, provide them with data related to stocks, sports, or pop culture. See the *Scenario Cards* for grades 6–8 specific scenarios.

Scenario Cards

Directions: Distribute the cards to students as appropriate and have them create the details of the scenarios they will perform from the information on the cards.

Grades K–2

Your friend spilled a box of crayons on the floor and has asked you to help pick them up. Some of the crayons have rolled under the table. The box holds 10 crayons. You pick up 7 crayons and put them in the box. How many more crayons do you need to find under the table? Discuss with your friend as you search for crayons.

You are buying muffins that come in packs of 3, 4, and 5. You must decide how to buy 10 muffins. What will you do?

You and your brother are at the store and have just discovered a new robot that lights up, talks, and walks. You have saved $12. The cost of the robot is $25. How much more money do you need to save? Make a plan to convince your parents to pay you to do chores around the house to get the rest of the cash you need. Practice the pitch you will use with your parents, including the pay you should receive for each chore. Which chores will you need to complete to get enough money to buy the robot? Demonstrate scenes in which you imagine you are doing the chores and earning the cash you need.

Scenario Cards *(cont.)*

Grades 3–5

You woke up late for school this morning. It's 7:30 A.M. now. It takes you 20 minutes to eat breakfast, 5 minutes to brush your teeth, and 10 minutes to walk to the bus stop. Will you be able to make the 8 A.M. bus? Your mother is at your door, and she is quite upset. You need to tell her how you will adjust your schedule to make the bus and calm her down!

Your older sister is bragging about how much money she made babysitting and said, "I made $40 for babysitting for one night!" You know that the going rate is $5 an hour. How long were the parents gone if the amount of pay is right?

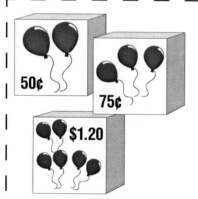

You and your sister are buying 10 balloons for a party. You each have a different idea of which package to buy. What conversation might you have? How will you persuade her that you are right?

Scenario Cards *(cont.)*

Grades 6–8

The local sports store is having a blowout sale where everything is reduced by 30%. You have a coupon for $10 off. About how much will you save if you buy a new baseball mitt that costs $89? Your dad just covered the cost of your baseball uniform and is not interested in spending more. Convince your dad that this is the moment to buy!

Several sports clubs have a special offer, and you are trying to decide which club to join. You have found three clubs that have facilities that you like. The Play It Now Club charges a $100 joining fee and $4 per visit. The My Fit Club charges $6 per visit with no joining fee. The Health Plus Club charges a $50 joining fee and $5 per visit. Which club should you join? Why might someone else make a different choice?

You run 2 miles every day. You ran on Monday and averaged 5.8 minutes per mile. On Tuesday, you had an even better run, averaging 5.6 minutes per mile. Wednesday, you ate an entire large pizza just before running and only averaged 6.8 minutes per mile. Your coach told you that you must average 6-minute miles over the course of the week. Share your plan to meet this goal over the next two days with your coach. Convince the coach that you can do it.

Monologue

Model Lesson: The Life of a Shape

Model Lesson Overview

There are often monologues in stories and plays that illuminate what a character is thinking. Most often, the monologue reveals a conflict of some kind that the character is wrestling with, a choice to be made, or a problem to be solved. Mathematical monologues give students the opportunity to personify a mathematical concept. Students may create monologues that are dramatic, comedic, or a combination of both. The properties of shapes are highlighted in this presentation, but any mathematical concept is appropriate to consider.

Standards

K–2

- Understands basic properties of simple geometric shapes and similarities and differences between simple geometric shapes

- Understands the common language of spatial sense

- Uses variations of locomotor and nonlocomotor movement and vocal pitch, tempo, and tone for different characters

3–5

- Knows basic geometric language for describing and naming shapes

- Understands basic properties of figures

- Uses variations of locomotor and nonlocomotor movement and vocal pitch, tempo, and tone for different characters

6–8

- Understands the relationships between two- and three-dimensional representations of a figure

- Understands how descriptions, dialogue, and actions are used to discover, articulate, and justify character motivation

Materials

- Monologue examples from familiar sources

- *Monologue Example: Cube* (page 101, monologueexample.pdf)

- Chart paper

- *Monologue Planner* (page 102, monologueplanner.pdf)

Monologue *(cont.)*

Preparation

Select a number of shapes for students to use in their monologues. Decide whether you want to assign shapes to specific students or let them choose their own shapes.

Read over *Monologue Example: Cube* (page 101) so that you can present it with dramatic interest. You may also wish to select an example of a monologue from literature to share with students. Other ideas are provided in the Specific Grade Level Ideas.

Procedure

1. If students are not familiar with what a monologue is, share a monologue from a familiar play, a movie, or a book, or a monologue that has been written for children. Talk with students about how a monologue is different from a dialogue.

2. Read the *Monologue Example: Cube* (page 101) to students *without* dramatic flair. Ask students to identify the dilemma or problem that the cube is sharing. Next, reread the monologue again without expression, asking students to close their eyes and visualize the character. How might the cube look, talk, move, or behave? Give students a copy of the monologue and ask them to consider how it could be read dramatically. For example, when might they change their voice, make a gesture, move, pause, or otherwise dramatize the reading?

3. Provide time for students to practice delivering the monologue in pairs. Invite students to share their performances with the whole class.

4. Assign a shape to each student or have students select their own. Have students form groups with others who are working with the same shape. Provide each group with chart paper, and direct groups to brainstorm and record ideas related to their shape. If desired, use the Group Brainstorming Questions to help stimulate ideas.

5. Once a few of minutes have passed, direct groups to read their list of ideas and think about which ideas suggest a conflict, which ideas could lead to effective dramatization, and which ideas might suggest humor. Have students share their thinking with their groups and discuss possible ideas to develop into a monologue.

6. Provide time for students to develop their monologues in class or at home using the *Monologue Planner* (page 102). Share the *Monologue Example: Cube* with students to help them see the connection between the planning process and the final product. Use the Planning Questions to help guide students.

Monologue *(cont.)*

7. Invite students to present their monologues to the class.

8. Debrief the monologues. Ask questions such as "What mathematical insights did you gain? What emotions did you feel? What aspects of shape did your character focus on? How did you suggest your character's personality?"

Group Brainstorming Questions

- What do you think of when you see this shape?

- What properties does this shape have?

- What makes this shape useful?

- How will your character bring to life the characteristics of the shape?

Planning Questions

- If this shape were a person, what personality traits might you associate with it? Why?

- How old is your character? Where does he or she live? What does he or she like/dislike?

- What dilemma does the character have?

- What is your character trying to persuade us about?

- What gestures would suggest this shape?

- How does the shape feel about what it is saying? What facial expressions and body stances would portray this feeling?

- How will your voice change during the monologue?

- What costume might you wear to help us imagine the character?

Monologue *(cont.)*

Specific Grade Level Ideas

K–2

This activity can be more improvisational for younger students. When you give students a specific context, it helps them to consider how their character would react in that situation. Assign students a shape, and ask them to imagine they are entering a party where nobody knows them. How would they introduce themselves as a triangle, a square, or a circle? What is important about how they look, where they can be found, or what their life is like? Students can begin their monologues by saying, "Hi, I'm (name of shape). Let me tell you a bit about myself." Students can also pretend to be a particular number.

3–5

Students may choose to memorize their monologues and put on a show for invited guests. Help them practice improvising if they forget their exact lines. You can also allow them to write their monologues or make notes that will trigger their thinking on index cards so that memorizing the lines doesn't become more important than the exploration of character. Through rehearsal, students will become familiar with their lines and be able to rely less on the index cards, but having them available may help the performers relax as they share their work. Students can also pretend to be a particular number or unit of measure.

Monologue *(cont.)*

6–8

Assign two- and three-dimensional shapes to students. Invite students with related shapes to present back-to-back in order to facilitate a discussion about similarities and differences. Or you can emphasize the platonic solids. Students can also focus on a particular number, measurement unit, measure of central tendency, or distribution display.

Identify a key emotion or feeling for students to connect to the monologue such as longing, fear, or being misunderstood. For example, ellipse-shaped objects may feel misunderstood as they are seen by too many as only a stretched out circle or as lacking singular focus because of their two foci. A triangle, for example, may long to turn into a cone or to be similar to another triangle, or a cylinder may fear losing its faces and turning into a tube. Challenge students to really think about the "life" of their shape (e.g., a circular-shape monologue could reference the dilemma of never being able to stand still without rolling or falling down, the magnificence of pi, or the need to serve as a sewer cover because the top can't fall down the hole).

Monologue Example: Cube

I love that so much about me is the same size. I mean, I can wear my clothes any way I want. I can put my tops on the bottom and my bottoms on the top. And I adore my right angles. They fit together so well. I mean, if I get together with my cube friends, we can make a wall and none of us have to stand upside down or sideways! And how about my symmetry? There are four different ways that my faces can fold themselves in half and match perfectly.

Sometimes, I think my other-shaped friends are jealous of me. I think they wish they had my properties, too. But I'm going to confide in you. The thing is, sometimes I wish I were just a bit more irregular, a bit more mixed up! I mean, what would it be like to see a whole different side of yourself just by looking at a different face or edge? Or what if you weren't always being called on to make walls and had a bit more free time? Really, the thing I wrestle with most is...dare I say it? Why can't I think "outside the box?" Sometimes I feel like a blockhead!

Name _____ Date _____

Monologue Planner

Directions: Fill in the planner to help you create your monologue.

Properties:	Things this reminds me of:	Facts about my character:

Math Topic:

My character's personality:	What my character wants or is bothered by:	Ways I can add drama (use of voice, gesture, props):

Music

#51088—Strategies to Integrate the Arts in Mathematics

Music

Understanding Music

Music has played a significant role in every culture since the beginning of time. Now with recent technology, our favorite tunes are readily available to us, and music has become even more prevalent in our lives. Dr. Howard Gardner has identified musical intelligence as one form of intelligence (2011). His theory of multiple intelligence suggests that students learn in different ways, and for some students, connecting with rhythm, beat, and melody provides access to learning. And as any adult who has introduced a cleanup song knows, music can motivate children and help them make transitions from one activity to another. Recently, attention has been given to the benefits of music in academic performance. It has been suggested that early music training develops language skills, spatial relations, and memory (Perret and Fox 2006).

Music and mathematics have long been linked. After all, it was the famous mathematician Pythagoras who first noted that the pitch of a string was directly related to its length. "Mathematics is also universal, crosses cultural, historical, and intellectual boundaries, and is reflected in music. The interconnectedness of math and music pulsates with a rhythm and harmony of its own" (Garland and Kahn 1995).

In the following strategies, students explore mathematical ideas alongside the basic elements of music. Students engage in singing, playing, and composing music as well as using everyday objects as nontraditional instruments. The focus is on deepening mathematical knowledge while experiencing the joy of creating music together in ways that all students can participate. Along the way, students develop a deeper understanding of and skills in creating music. No previous musical training is needed for you or your students.

Exploring mathematical ideas through music engages and motivates students. As students identify, apply, and generalize ideas to real-world situations, mathematics becomes meaningful and purposeful. Abstract ideas are connected to concrete models, and students' representational fluency deepens. The more avenues we provide for students to experience mathematics, the more likely we are to connect with the variable ways in which students learn.

Music (cont.)

Strategies for Music

❧ Found Sounds

Sounds are all around us; they are found when we attend to them or manipulate them. Think about the sound of light rain or the squeals of delight you hear near a playground. There is rhythm in these sounds. Composer R. Murray Schafer thinks about the world as a musical composition. He notes, "In [music] we try to get people to use their senses to listen carefully, to look carefully" (quoted in New 2009). What makes a sound music rather than noise may depend on the listener, but it is also related to pitch (high or low) and rhythm. When students collect found sounds, they gain a new appreciation for what music is. They can also better understand the environment from which sounds come. Students can categorize these sounds, experiment with making them, and explore their dynamics (volume). Their findings can be represented in graphs.

❧ Songwriting

When students sing, a deep connection is created with the melody, rhythm, and lyrics of a song. Further, creating and making music supports academic achievement (Deasy 2002). Though students have opportunities to sing in school, far less attention is given to their ability to create their own songs. This strategy invites students to become songwriters, and as they do, they become more familiar with the importance of tone, rhythm, and beat. Students can begin on an intuitive level or simplify the task, for example, by creating new lyrics for a song they already know. As songs can help us to remember things, these adaptations can help students to retain important mathematical information. Also, writing lyrics will prompt students to discuss, synthesize, and categorize curricular concepts. Students can explore rhythms on a drum or experiment with notes on a keyboard. As their musical knowledge expands, they can create original melodies as well as score their compositions.

❧ Scoring

When music is composed, it needs to be scored so that others can perform it. Scoring is the communication of the sounds that are to be made and the timing of those sounds. The scoring can be done in nontraditional ways so that all learners are able to participate; for example, students can record a word in writing, such as *clap*, or draw a hand to indicate when such a sound is to be made. Such scoring techniques allow students to construct the symbols and their meaning. Traditional scoring can also be considered, allowing students to experiment with the common language of musicians. "Musical elements such as steady beat, rhythm, tempo, volume, melody, and harmony possess inherent mathematical concepts such as spatial properties, sequencing, counting, patterning, and one-to-one correspondence" (Geist and Geist 2008).

Music (*cont.*)

∾ Call-and-Response

Used for centuries around the world, call-and-response is a musical pattern of phrases exchanged between musicians. There is a conversational pattern with the second musician (the "response") responding to the first musician (the "call"). This pattern has rich cultural roots in African, African American, Indian classical, and Cuban traditions among others. In the United States, such songs are most familiar as sea chanteys and maritime work songs.

The cadences and rhythmic patterns involve learners and support memory. This strategy supports full participation as students pose and answer questions in an engaging way to review information, reinforce skills, and expand ideas (Plessinger 2012).

∾ Chants

Chants involve the rhythmic repetition of sounds or words. They can be sung or spoken. They can be a component of spiritual practices or heard on a football field. By combining different dynamics (ranging from soft to loud), pitch (variations from high to low), and different notes (length of duration), students can create engaging sound effects that help them learn and remember ideas. According to Sonja Dunn (1999), "A chant is a rhythmic group recitation." Chants can be used in a variety of ways. They can be created with catchy rhythms that make the associated words easy to learn and remember. When this form of chants is emphasized, students retain important mathematical information. Chants also can be constructed by layering phrases on top of another that are then spoken or sung simultaneously. In this format, the use of differing rhythms and pitch create interest and suggest relationships among the chosen phrases and thus the content being considered.

Found Sounds

Model Lesson: Categorization

Model Lesson Overview

Students listen closely to the sounds around them, think about the sounds that they can make with common objects, and categorize those sounds according to variations in loudness, or *dynamics*, and other properties of sound. Students bring in a "found sound" from home and consider the dynamics of these sounds as well as their other properties. They conduct a survey focused on one property, represent their findings in graphs, and summarize their findings.

Standards

K–2	3–5
• Collects and represents information about objects or events in simple graphs • Knows standard symbols used to notate dynamics	• Organizes and displays data in simple bar graphs, pie charts, and line graphs • Knows symbols and traditional terms referring to dynamics
6–8	**9–12**
• Organizes and displays data using tables, graphs, frequency distributions, and plots • Understands the basic concepts of center and dispersion of data • Knows standard notation symbols for dynamics	• Selects and uses the best method of representing and describing a set of data • Uses the elements of music for expressive effects (e.g., pitch, rhythm, harmony, dynamics, timbre, texture, form)

Materials

- Various household items that produce sound (athletic shoes that squeak, utensils to rub together, etc.)

- *Characteristics of Sound* (page 113, characteristicssound.pdf)

- *Music Graph* (page 114, musicgraph.pdf)

- Copies of a class list (one per pair of students)

Found Sounds (cont.)

Preparation

Tell students that they are to collect sounds for homework. Their job is to find objects that make interesting and different sounds and bring them to class the next day. Each student should bring one or two items. Provide examples of items they could find, such as an athletic shoe that squeaks, kitchen utensils that could be struck and rubbed against each other, or tinfoil to be crunched. You should also gather a couple of items to add variety to the collection or to give to students who may forget to bring one. Other ideas are provided in the Specific Grade Level Ideas.

Decide how you will display the Dynamics Chart (see Step 3 of Procedure) and prepare accordingly.

Procedure

1. Have students share their found sounds. Provide time for students to experiment with the "instruments" in small groups and explore different ways they can be used to make sounds. Encourage students to find more than one way to make a sound with each item. For example, they can blow on the top of a bottle, shake it with pennies or pebbles inside, or roll it. Provide time for students to share their discoveries about new ways to make sounds.

2. After each instrument is played, ask students to suggest adjectives to describe the sound it makes. If students are aware of the categorization of orchestral instruments, ask, "What instrument does this remind you of that you might hear in an orchestra or band? What type of instrument is this?" For example, a student might compare plucking an elastic band pulled taut around a piece of cardboard to playing a banjo or he or she might compare blowing on a bottle top to a wind instrument.

3. Introduce the word *dynamics* as the term musicians use to describe variations of loudness. Tell students that dynamics is one property of sound. Display the following chart that lists some Italian terms used to describe the loudness of western approaches to music.

Dynamics Chart

Word	Meaning	Symbol
Fortissimo	Very loud	*ff*
Forte	Loud	*f*
Mezzo forte	Moderately loud	*mf*
Mezzo piano	Moderately soft	*mp*
Piano	Soft	*p*
Pianissimo	Very soft	*pp*

Found Sounds *(cont.)*

4. Have students practice saying the Italian terms and explain that these words describe or identify the different volumes. Have a few volunteers play their instruments with different dynamics. Point out to students that these terms are relative. In other words, what is forte on one instrument may be softer than forte on another instrument. For example, a piano will sound louder than a violin even though both might be playing at a forte level. The same is true for twisting a cap and scrunching a plastic bag. Ask students to identify sounds with dynamics that do not change, such as an alarm clock ringing.

5. Have students work in small groups to categorize their instruments according to dynamics.

6. Distribute *Characteristics of Sound* (page 113) to students and point out that the property of dynamics has already been provided as an example of a property of sound. Have students brainstorm other properties of sound. These can include a wide range of possibilities, including material (plastic, natural, metal), pitch (high, low), duration (time the sound lasts, sustained or intermittent), and sound-production method (tapping, rolling, hitting, shaking, blowing air, or plucking). As students identify a property, record it for students to refer to throughout the lesson, and have them record it in the first column of the sheet.

7. Once students list a property, have them brainstorm words that describe or identify ways that property could vary. Have students record these words in the second column.

8. Tell students to choose one of the instruments they brought to class and identify the words in the chart that could describe the sounds it can make. Have students circle these terms on their recording sheet.

9. Have students find partners and distribute *Music Graph* (page 114) to each pair. Direct students to choose one of the properties listed, identify the descriptors they will use, and record this information on the sheet. Have students survey their classmates to determine which of their chosen descriptors students used to describe their instruments. Give students a copy of a class list to help them keep track of whom they have surveyed.

10. On the recording sheet, have students create a graph of their data and write their findings. Then, have students share their graphs. As they do so, ask follow-up questions. Use the Questions for Discussion to guide the conversation.

11. If time allows, have students experiment with ways to combine their sounds to create a musical composition.

Found Sounds (cont.)

Questions for Discussion

- What descriptors did you choose? Are there others that could be considered?

- How many more of our instruments were (name a descriptor) than (name a different descriptor)?

- What graph should we look at to find the number of instruments that were made from metal?

- What types of sounds were most common?

- Which sounds do you prefer? Why?

- If you were to create a musical composition, what sounds would you pick to be played together?

Specific Grade Level Ideas

K–2

Focusing on the terms *forte* and *piano*, have students practice making loud and soft sounds. For their surveys, have students choose only two to four descriptors for the sound property they choose. Ask several questions that require them to look at the information on the graph and add or subtract to find the answer.

As a follow-up activity, take students outside to listen for sounds. The sound outing could be to the cafeteria, to a city street, or to a secluded area. After listening for a couple of minutes, have students talk about the sounds they heard and how they could be categorized. Students can also use found sounds to model addition facts.

3–5

Students can explore the activity as written. Students will similarly benefit from a sound outing as described in the K–2 Specific Grade Level Ideas. They may also be interested in finding out their classmates' favorite songs and classifying those songs by artist or type of music. Students can also use found sounds to model multiplication facts.

Found Sounds (cont.)

6–8

Encourage students to represent their data in circle graphs and report their findings in fractions and percents.

You can expand the terms used to describe dynamics by including *pianississimo*, which means extremely soft and is represented by *ppp*; *fortississimo*, which means extremely loud and is represented by *fff*; *sforzando*, which means with a strong and sudden accent and is represented by *sfz*; *crescendo*, which means a gradual increase in volume and is represented by <; and *decrescendo*, which means a gradual decrease in volume and is represented by >. Have students listen to a piece of music, note the dynamics, and relate them to these terms. Students can also play their sounds together to further explore dynamics within combinations of sounds.

As a follow-up activity, students can do research about popular music. For example, they can represent the age of popular artists in box plots. Ask questions to highlight measures of central tendency and variation.

Students can also use found sounds to model proportional relationships.

9–12

Have students collect sounds from found instruments, the Internet, and the environment. Then, have them categorize the changes in tempo or beats per minute (BPM). Students can then create a recording of sounds that includes a variety of changes in tempo (e.g., increasing at a constant rate, increasing at an increasing rate, or increasing at a decreasing rate). Have students play their recordings while listeners graph the change in tempo over time.

Name _____ Date _____

Characteristics of Sound

Directions: In the first column, write properties of sound. In the second column, list words that can be used to describe or identify sounds for each property. An example has been done for you. Then, write the name of your instrument and circle each word that describes it.

My Instrument: _____

Property	Words to Describe or Identify
dynamics	pianissimo, piano, mezzo piano, mezzo forte, forte, fortissimo

Name _____   Date _____

Music Graph

Directions: Complete each task.

1. The property we chose is:

   _____

2. The words to describe or identify for this property we will include are:

   _____

   _____

3. Our graph:

4. Our findings:

   _____

   _____

   _____

   _____

Songwriting

Model Lesson: Adaptation

Model Lesson Overview

Students express mathematical knowledge by writing new lyrics to familiar songs. The result is sometimes called a *piggyback song* as it is built or rides on a song that already exists. Adapted songs can be simple (one verse) or involve several verses separated by a repeating chorus. In such cases, the chorus can represent central ideas worth repeating, and the verses can be constructed to expand ideas, consider different examples, or suggest a sequence. In this strategy, students explore an adapted song and then create their own.

Standards

K–2

- Uses base-ten concepts to compare whole-number relationships
- Sings ostinatos (repetition of a short musical pattern)

3–5

- Understands the correct order of operations for performing arithmetic computations
- Sings on pitch and in rhythm, with appropriate timbre, diction, and posture, and maintains a steady tempo

6–8

- Understands special values of patterns, relationships, and functions
- Sings with good breath control, expression, and technical accuracy at a level that includes modest ranges and changes of tempo, key, and meter

Materials

- *Song Exemplar* (page 119, songexemplar.pdf)
- *Lyric Brainstorming Guide* (page 120, lyricbrainstorm.pdf)
- *Chorus and Verses* (page 121, chorusverses.pdf)

Songwriting *(cont.)*

Preparation

Decide how you will group students as they plan for their song adaptations. Identify the mathematical theme of the song on which you would like the groups to focus. Refer to the *Song Exemplar* (page 119) for your grade level to familiarize yourself with these models. Other ideas are provided in the Specific Grade Level Ideas.

Procedure

1. Tell students that they are going to adapt a song to incorporate the facts and ideas they have learned and identify the mathematical focus. Sing or have students sing the *Song Exemplar* (page 119) for your grade level as a model.

2. Distribute the *Lyric Brainstorming Guide* (page 120) to students. As a class, brainstorm key ideas and descriptive phrases or instructions that students may like to include in their lyrics related to the content you have selected. Have students record this information using the *Lyric Brainstorming Guide*.

3. Have students go back through the list and regroup their ideas into categories, recording their thinking on the *Lyric Brainstorming Guide*. This categorization can help organize the lyrics. During this process, encourage students to decide what lyrics are most relevant and what lyrics may be too tangential to include.

4. Ask students to brainstorm familiar songs that might be used for the melody. These can include childhood songs, holiday songs, songs they have heard on the radio or online, or advertising jingles. Brainstorm songs that everyone in the class knows, keeping in mind students who may have different traditions and consequently may not be as familiar with some of the songs. Do not overlook obvious songs, such as "If You're Happy and You Know It Clap Your Hands," "This Land Is Your Land," or "Itsy Bitsy Spider." The songs will take on new meaning once the words have been changed.

5. Focus on some of the key terms and brainstorm rhyming words, having students record them on the *Lyric Brainstorming Guide*. However, remind students that not all lines have to rhyme and that sometimes it is repeated words and rhythm that make a song work.

6. Introduce the terms *chorus* and *verse.* Ask students to think about the structure of the song "Old MacDonald." Explain that the lines about the different animals are verses and the repeated phrase "Old MacDonald had a farm, E-I-E-I-O" is the chorus. Ask students to identify what core idea(s) might be included in a chorus so that it is repeated throughout the song.

Songwriting *(cont.)*

7. Have the class try a few different melodies until they find one that fits the content in both mood and in the rhythm of the words. Pick a few lines from the *Lyric Brainstorming Guide* that might work and try them with each melody to identify the right fit. Encourage students to use the same structure that the song uses in terms of rhythm and number of syllables. In some cases, they might elongate a syllable or adjust their singing of syllables to make the rhythm work.

8. At this point, students can work in small groups to complete their adaptation. If they are including a chorus and two verses in their adaptation, distribute *Chorus and Verses* (page 121) and have them complete it. They can then refer to it as they sing their song. As they work, use the Planning Questions to support their thinking.

9. Provide time for groups to share and discuss their songs.

Planning Questions

- Are there other mathematical ideas that you could include?
- When might we use this math in a real-world situation?
- What could you do to help you think of a rhyming word?
- Does it make sense to keep some of the lines from the original song?
- Have you checked to make sure your new lyrics match the structure of the original song?
- Is there a word you could add (or take away) to make the rhythm work better?

Specific Grade Level Ideas

K–2

As a class, brainstorm ideas to create lyrics and adapt a simple song that students know well. Work with students to learn the song and sing it together. Topics may include counting songs, shapes, or addition and subtraction. Short songs can be used that don't require multiple verses and a chorus. Consider the *Song Exemplar* and share the Grades K–2 *Song Exemplar* with students as a model. Students can use their hands to demonstrate the changes in number as they sing, and the song can continue to higher places with the trading theme of the song.

Songwriting *(cont.)*

3–5

Students can create a song to help them remember rules such as the order of operations. Such a song may only contain one verse and a chorus. Note that students often use a mnemonic device to remember this order, such as **P**lease **E**xcuse **M**y **D**ear **A**unt **S**ally (**p**arentheses, **e**xponents, **m**ultiply and **d**ivide, **a**dd and **s**ubtract). Unfortunately, the result is that they may conclude incorrectly. For example, they may think that they must multiply before they divide and add before they subtract. Consider the adaptation of "Jingle Bells" in the Grades 3–5 *Song Exemplar*. It emphasizes the left-to-right component of the convention; for example, you add or subtract in the order the operations occur from left to right. You can teach students this song as a way to remind them of this important fact. Then, students can create other songs for vocabulary or procedures they need to remember. When students help to write the song, they synthesize and express their knowledge through the creation of lyrics.

Students can also explore conceptual ideas. For instance, students can create an adaptation that focuses on what to do with remainders, something that many students find challenging. Students can begin with a stanza that provides an example of when the remainder can be divided into fractional parts. Students can then create other verses that describe a situation in which remainders are omitted or one in which they are rounded up to the next whole number. Remind students that they can create a chorus to sing after each verse.

6–8

Students can explore ideas for lyrics and song melodies to be used. They can find and download popular songs and lyrics from the Internet. Listening to them and seeing the words may help students to replace the words and to identify the patterns of the rhythm.

For the Grades 6–8 *Song Exemplar*, have students use gestures to indicate the directions of the slope as uphill (from left to right), downhill (from right to left), horizontal, or vertical.

Song Exemplar

Grades K–2

Sung to "She'll Be Coming 'Round the Mountain"

She'll be trading her 10 ones when she has 'em
She'll be trading her 10 ones when she has 'em
She'll be trading her 10 ones
She'll be trading her 10 ones
She'll be trading her 10 ones for 1 ten

Grades 3–5

Sung to "Jingle Bells" (Starting with *Dashing through the snow…*)

We must all agree
On the order to compute
Otherwise you see
We might pay too much loot
Follow the same rule
Working left to right
What fun it is to use this tool
An equation done just right

Oh, left to right, left to right
Whatever you first see
Powers and parentheses
In the order that they be
Left to right, left to right
Multiply, divide
Left to right, add, subtract
We do it all in stride.

Grades 6–8

Sung to "Three Blind Mice"

(Chorus)
Rise over run
Rise over run
What is the slope?
What is the slope?

(Verse 1)
With negative slope
It goes downhill
Like a bank account
After paying bills
Take the change in y
Over the change in x
To find the slope

(Verse 2)
With positive slope
It goes uphill
Like the water's height
In a glass you fill
Take the change in y
Over the change in x
To find the slope

(Verse 3)
Horizontal lines
Have a zero slope
With vertical lines
Its undefined slope
Take the change in y
Over the change in x
To find the slope

Name _____ Date _____

Lyric Brainstorming Guide

Directions: Use the chart to help you plan your song lyrics.

Math Concept:	
Key Ideas to Include:	**Descriptive Phrases or Instructions:**
Categories:	**Potential Rhymes:**

Name _____ Date _____

Chorus and Verses

Directions: Use the chart to help you plan your song structure.

Title of Song

Chorus

Verse 1

Verse 2

Scoring

Model Lesson: Clock Music

Model Lesson Overview

In this strategy, students work together to identify a variety of sounds, such as tapping a pencil on a desk and rubbing your feet on the floor, and then play the sounds at particular intervals within a one-minute time limit. Students must create a score to remember the choices they make about the sounds they will use and when the sounds will occur during the minute interval. The mathematical emphasis is on counting, the second hand on a clock, multiplication and division, and fractions.

Standards

K-2

- Understands the concept of a unit and its subdivision into equal parts

- Uses a variety of sound sources when composing

3-5

- Understands basic number theory concepts (e.g., factors, multiples, divisibility)

- Creates and arranges short songs and instrumental pieces within specified guidelines

6-8

- Understands the relationships among equivalent number representations and the advantages and disadvantages of each type of representation

- Uses a variety of traditional and nontraditional sound sources when composing and arranging

Materials

- Large analog clock with a second hand

- *Individual Musical Score* (page 126, musicscore.pdf)

Scoring *(cont.)*

Preparation

Draw a large clock (without hands but with numbers and minute marks) on the board. Leave enough room to record a key or legend. Refer to the Specific Grade Level Ideas for additional ideas.

Procedure

1. Ask students to think about different ways a minute can be separated into equal intervals of time (e.g., 60 intervals of 1 second, 2 intervals of 30 seconds, 3 intervals of 20 seconds, and so forth). Provide time for students to work with neighbors to identify possibilities. Record students' responses, taking suggestions from students such as, "Let's play something once every five seconds." Tell students that as a class, they will create a composition highlighting these different durations of time.

2. Show students the analog clock and have them clap out the seconds with the second hand for one minute. Have them identify sounds other than clapping that they might make, such as tapping the desk with a ruler. Once students decide on a sound that everyone can make, ask them to come up with a simple symbol that will represent the sound of that "instrument." Mark the symbol (e.g., *R* for *tapping ruler*) outside each of the minute marks on the drawn clock to indicate when the instrument is to be played within the one-minute interval.

3. Tell students that they also need a key to help them remember the meanings of the symbols. In a corner by the drawn clock, record *R* and *tapping ruler.*

4. Ask students to identify another time interval from their list. Again, have students identify an instrument and a symbol. Record this in the appropriate positions around the clock and add the information to the key. Have students practice making the sound at the correct intervals as they watch the analog clock. Repeat for two to four more time intervals.

5. Divide the class into the appropriate number of sections and assign each of them one of the "instruments." Point out to students that they are sitting in sections and responsible for playing their parts like members of an orchestra. Distribute the *Individual Musical Score* (page 126) and have them make a score that only shows their assigned part. Have groups practice their parts a few times.

Scoring *(cont.)*

6. Remind students to sit where they can see the analog clock so that they know when their parts should be played. Tell students to begin their performance when the second hand reaches the 12. Though you can act as a conductor and point to a section to signal that they are about to play, encourage students to watch the clock in order to determine when they should play their instruments. Have students perform their composition a few times for practice.

7. Suggest that at the 60-second mark, all players create a special sound as the culminating moment of the piece, such as slamming a book closed, and have students practice making that sound once. Have students add this ending to their *Individual Musical Score*.

8. Perform the complete piece two or three times through and then use the Questions for Discussion to help students reflect on the experience.

Questions for Discussion

- How did the score help you to perform?

- What did you find challenging about the performance?

- What might you change if you were to play it again?

- What are other ways a conductor leads an orchestra? (when to play softly, loudly, or to stop playing) What hand signals might we use for these directions?

- If you played for 32 seconds, what intervals might you use for striking your beat?

- When were the greatest number of instruments playing? (All intervals are a factor of 60, so all instruments were playing at that time.)

- Without a score, how could we predict when more than one section would be playing? (Examine the common multiples of the factors of 60.)

Scoring *(cont.)*

Specific Grade Level Ideas

K–2

Students can practice counting by ones around the drawn clock as well as skip counting by fives and tens. A few students may suggest 30-second or 15-second intervals based on visual familiarity with a clock face or ways to divide a circle into halves or fourths. Limit the number of instrumental parts to four or fewer.

3–5

After students experience this activity, they can develop their own scores in small groups and perform them for the class, providing their own conductor. Students can also experiment with an interval longer than 60 seconds, perhaps indicated on a number line or with a circle drawn for each minute, to gain additional practice identifying all factor pairs and using common multiples to predict when different sounds will be played at the same time.

6–8

Encourage students to create their own scores, distribute them to the class, and conduct their performance. Extend the mathematics in the activity by asking questions such as, "What fraction (or percent) of the time is the (name instrument) playing? For what fraction (or percent) of the composition is only one instrument playing?"

Name _____ Date _____

Individual Musical Score

Directions: Write the musical score for your part in the performance. Be sure to complete the key.

Key

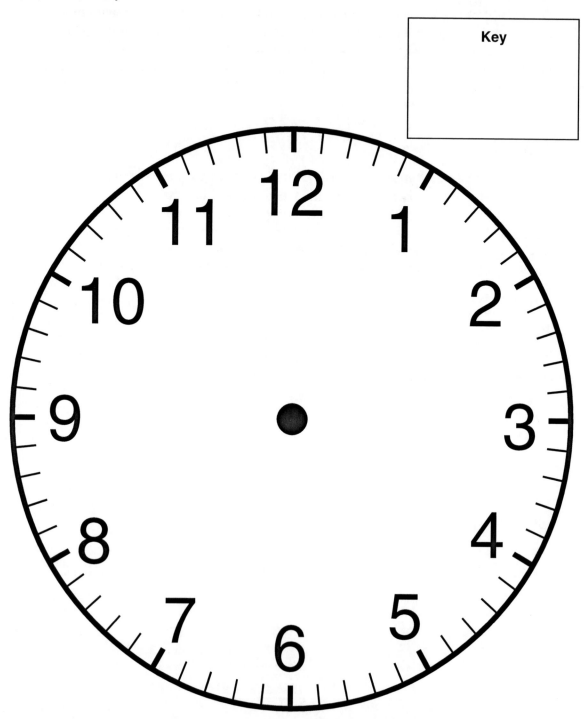

Call-and-Response

Model Lesson: Answer Me In Rhythm

Model Lesson Overview

This strategy reinforces mathematical ideas and engages students in testing their knowledge by posing questions and answering them in a rhythmic pattern. Call-and-response encourages collaboration and group problem solving. Students will work in pairs to create their own call-and-response song to demonstrate their knowledge about mathematical content. The focus is on equivalence, but this strategy can be used with any content.

Standards

K-2

- Knows processes for telling time, counting money, and measuring length, weight, and temperature, using basic standard and non-standard units

- Identifies simple music forms when presented aurally

3-5

- Selects and uses appropriate units of measurement, according to type and size of unit

- Uses specific strategies to estimate quantities and measurements

- Knows music of various styles representing diverse cultures

6-8

- Understands the relationships among linear dimensions, area, and volume and the corresponding uses of units, square units, and cubic units of measure

- Selects and uses appropriate estimation techniques to solve real-world problems

- Understands how the elements of music are used in various genres and cultures

9-12

- Uses trigonometric ratio methods to solve mathematical and real-world problems

- Understands how the elements of music and expressive devices are used in music from diverse genres and cultures

Call-and-Response (cont.)

Materials

- *Call-and-Response Examples* (page 131, callresponse.pdf)
- *Planning Chart for Call-and-Response* (page 132, callresponseplan.pdf)

Preparation

Decide how to break students into small groups. Practice a military-like cadence for the call-and-response examples given on *Call-and-Response Examples* (page 131), or create examples of your own. Note that the first example is simply recall and can be used to reinforce the ability to remember facts. In the second example, the caller should take a step while singing the first call, and the responder has to estimate before making a response. Other ideas are provided in the Specific Grade Level Ideas.

Procedure

1. Share examples of call-and-response (maritime cadences, work songs, sea chanteys, etc.), and discuss the historical and cultural aspects of this musical form. Ask older students, "What purpose did this form of music serve?" Younger students can respond to the question, "How is this way of singing like a conversation?"

2. Display the *Call-and-Response Examples* (page 131) or use your own examples. Tell the group that you will sing/call the question and they will respond in the same rhythm and melody. Then, practice the call-and-response with students, using the examples.

3. Divide the class into two groups, one for call and one for response. Have students practice the call-and-response technique independently.

4. Organize students into small groups and tell them that they will create their own call-and-response. Note that students can organize their phrases in one of three ways: they can match the melody of a tune or sea chantey, organize their phrases within a certain number of beats, or find an interesting rhythm, much as they do with rap. Also note that a group of students can call the question—it's not limited to one leader.

5. Distribute the *Planning Chart for Call-and-Response* (page 132), and have students use it to plan their call-and-response. Tell students that rhyming is optional. Encourage each group to create up to five questions to call to the class. Use the Planning Questions to guide students' thinking.

6. Have students present their call-and-response plan to you in writing. Give students informal feedback, and have them revise as necessary.

Call-and-Response *(cont.)*

7. Give each group the opportunity to present and perform their call-and-response with the class.

8. Use the Questions for Discussion to guide students as they reflect.

Planning Questions

- What mathematical questions interest you?

- What math facts do you need to remember?

- How might you pose a question to generate a short, quick answer?

- How might you phrase a question so that it has an interesting rhythm?

- With what words might you end the question so that they are easy to rhyme?

Questions for Discussion

- What strategies did you use to create the right rhythm?

- What did you notice when the call-and-response was done with a group?

- What call-and-response might you use to help you remember a mathematical idea?

- What mathematics did you learn by participating in another group's call-and-response?

- How might you make your call-and-response even more mathematically interesting or challenging?

Specific Grade Level Ideas

K–2

Create group call-and-responses about shapes. For example, "How many sides to a triangle?" This could be followed by "Three sides to make that shape." You can also teach students a melody or rhythm and ask a series of basic-fact questions in the call-and-response format. Students can march in place as they sing responses or add gestures. Don't worry about having students rhyme at this age unless you are the one crafting both call and response.

Call-and-Response (cont.)

3–5

The activity can be used as written. Clapping the beats will help students to recognize and follow the rhythm. Questions about measurement can relate to length, volume, and mass. This technique could also be used for basic-fact practice and knowledge of geometric shapes.

6–8

Students can focus on more complex mathematical relationships, such as how a change in side length impacts perimeter, area, or volume, as well as more complex rhythms. They can also ask open-ended questions that can be called again and again until the responders run out of ideas. For instance, the question might be, "What can you tell me about slope?"

9–12

Students can use the call-and-response strategy to reinforce concepts related to the Pythagorean theorem or trigonometric ratios. They can also experiment with the rhythm of the call-and-response.

Call-and-Response Examples

Money

CALL: How many pennies in a dime?

RESPONSE: 10 pennies work out just fine

(repeat lines 1 and 2)

CALL: Money

RESPONSE: Money

CALL: Money

RESPONSE: Money

ALL: Know your money equivalents

Measurement

The caller should step while singing the first call, and the responder should estimate before making a response.

CALL: How many inches did I step?

RESPONSE: (number) inches you did step

(repeat lines 1 and 2)

CALL: Measurement

RESPONSE: Measurement

CALL: Measurement

RESPONSE: Measurement

ALL: Know your measures and estimate

Name _____ Date _____

Planning Chart for Call-and-Response

Directions: Complete the chart to plan your call-and-response.

Call: Possible Questions	Response: Possible Answers and Rhymes

Chants

Model Lesson: Length of Notes

Model Lesson Overview

Students investigate the duration of different musical notes, focusing on the role of fractions in music. Through a process of adding one layer or phrase on top of another in a chant, the different durations of the notes and the relations among them become particularly noticeable. To create the chants, students combine interesting phrases to be spoken/sung at the same time with different dynamics (ranging from soft to loud), pitch (low to high), and notes (short to long).

Standards

K-2

- Understands the concept of a unit and its subdivision into equal parts

- Knows standard symbols used to notate meter (e.g., $\frac{2}{4}$, $\frac{3}{4}$, $\frac{4}{4}$ time signatures) in simple patterns

3-5

- Understands the concepts related to fractions and decimals

- Knows standard symbols used to notate meter (e.g., $\frac{2}{4}$, $\frac{3}{4}$, $\frac{4}{4}$ time signatures) and rhythm (whole, half, quarter, eighth notes) in simple patterns

6-8

- Understands the characteristics and properties of the set of rational numbers and its subsets

- Uses standard notation to record musical ideas

Materials

- *Musical Score* (musicalscore.doc)

- *Chant Reflection* (page 139, chantreflection.pdf)

Preparation

Reflect on your students' understanding of fractions and how you might want to group them for this activity. If your school has a music teacher, talk with him or her about how you might connect this exploration with lessons or a musical piece within the music curriculum. Use the *Musical Score* (musicalscore.doc) to show to students, which is written in $\frac{4}{4}$ time, or select your own. As you preread the Procedure, think about where to display the initial words and diagrams so that others can be added. Other ideas are provided in the Specific Grade Level Ideas.

Chants (cont.)

Procedure

1. Write the following list of food items on the board so students can see them.

ravioli

sushi

soup

Have students say the words aloud as they clap the syllables. Record the number of syllables next to each word.

2. Explain to students that they are going to create a chant by saying these words at the same time, using the same amount of time. Have the whole group say "ravioli" as they clap out the four beats or syllables. Tell students that having four beats to one measure is common in music. Display the musical score written in $\frac{4}{4}$ time, and draw students' attention to the time signature and how the measures are identified.

3. On the board, draw a long horizontal line at a height that will allow two additional sections to be added. (You may wish to use the circle model with younger students. See the K–2 Specific Grade Level Ideas.) Tell students to think of this line as representing the time it took to say "ravioli" (the whole measure). Ask, "How many beats did this take?" *(4)* "How many beats did each syllable get?" *(1)* "What fraction of the whole measure did each syllable get?" ($\frac{1}{4}$) Divide the line into four equivalent segments, and write one of the syllables of *ravioli* below each segment along with the fractions. (See the following diagram.) Ask, "What number sentence could we write to show this?" ($\frac{1}{4} + \frac{1}{4} + \frac{1}{4} + \frac{1}{4} = 1$)

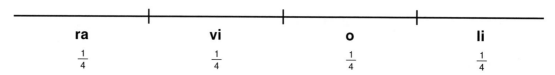

| ra | vi | o | li |
| $\frac{1}{4}$ | $\frac{1}{4}$ | $\frac{1}{4}$ | $\frac{1}{4}$ |

Chants *(cont.)*

4. Tell students, "We are going to say 'sushi' in the same amount of time as 'ravioli.'" Ask, "How many beats will we use?" *(4)* "How many beats will each syllable get?" *(2 beats)* "What fraction of the whole measure will each syllable get?" ($\frac{1}{2}$) Draw a second line, and write the syllables and fractions below. Ask, "What number sentence could we write to show this?" ($\frac{1}{2}$ + $\frac{1}{2}$ = 1)

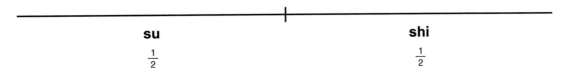

su	**shi**
$\frac{1}{2}$	$\frac{1}{2}$

5. Lead students in saying "sushi." Then, divide the class into two groups and have one group say "ravioli" while the other says "sushi." Have student groups repeat the phrases four times in a row, keeping the correct tempos.

6. Have students say "soup" in a drawn out manner, lasting four beats or claps, draw another line, and record the data.

soup

1

7. Divide the class into three groups. Have the first group say "ravioli." After that word is repeated twice, have the second group join in with "sushi," and after two repetitions of these words, direct the third group to join in with "soup." Once all three layers are included, have the whole group repeat the chant several times.

8. Now, write *corn tortillas and bean salad* and have students talk with a neighbor about how to represent this phrase on the line. Have students agree on what should be shown and record the new representation at the top of the expanded diagram. Ask, "What number sentence could we write to show this?" ($\frac{1}{8}$ + $\frac{1}{8}$ + $\frac{1}{8}$ + $\frac{1}{8}$ + $\frac{1}{8}$ + $\frac{1}{8}$ + $\frac{1}{8}$ + $\frac{1}{8}$ = 1)

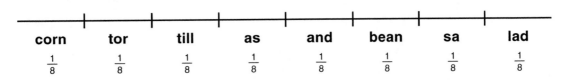

corn	**tor**	**till**	**as**	**and**	**bean**	**sa**	**lad**
$\frac{1}{8}$	$\frac{1}{8}$	$\frac{1}{8}$	$\frac{1}{8}$	$\frac{1}{8}$	$\frac{1}{8}$	$\frac{1}{8}$	$\frac{1}{8}$

9. Divide the class into four groups, and have students perform the four layers of the chant.

Chants *(cont.)*

10. Tell students that you will give each group time to elaborate on their layer of the chant. Use the Planning Questions to guide their thinking. When each group is prepared, have students practice their parts together and then present the chant. Ask, "What feedback could you give to other sections about the ways they embellished their part of the chant? What struck you about the sound and rhythms produced in the chants?"

11. Have students create their own chants. Tell students to identify a category of words that interests them and then to choose words to fit the beat. Distribute the *Chant Reflection* (page 139) for students to complete.

12. Invite a few students to share their explanations of how to use fractions to represent a phrase. Use the Questions for Discussion to further probe their thinking about fractions and music.

Planning Questions

- What pitch (high or low) do you want to use?

- How loud (dynamics) do you want to be?

- What other sound effects might you add to give your layer more interest (clapping, stomping, slapping the desk, and so forth)?

- Are there gestures you could add to emphasize your tempo (slow, curved motions or quick, jagged movements)?

Questions for Discussion

- Why are all the equations equal to 1?

- If we created a word bank to help us write our explanations, what words would we include?

- What do you notice about the fractions that are and are not used in music?

- How can you predict the number of times each layer of your chant will be repeated?

- Describe the effect of using words of different length, numbers of syllables, and tempos in order to create a layered chant.

Chants *(cont.)*

Specific Grade Level Ideas

K–2

Create a list of two or three food items, exploring wholes, halves, and/or fourths. Students don't need to record number sentences with the fractions. Some students will do better with a parts-of-the-whole circular model of fractions rather than a linear one. In such a model, the fractions would be represented as shown.

 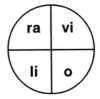

Lead students in creating their own chants using other types of foods or topics such as animals, names, or curricular topics.

3–5

To have students connect more formally to names of musical notes, you can also record the following on the diagram:

Whole note 𝗼

Half note ♩

Quarter note ♩

Eighth note ♪

One-sixteenth note ♬

Fifth-grade students can also explore the 6–8 Specific Grade Level Ideas.

Chants *(cont.)*

6–8

Students can experiment with alternating beats in addition to investigating steady beats. To do so, they would assign a variety of durations for different syllables within a word or phrase. For example, they can say or sing the words *chicken fricassee* by assigning the first three syllables a value of one beat, or quarter notes, and the last two syllables a value of one-half of a beat, or eighth notes. Students can then record the number sentence $\frac{1}{4} + \frac{1}{4} + \frac{1}{4} + \frac{1}{8} + \frac{1}{8} = 1$ to record this combination. Have students write equations to identify 10 different ways (different order doesn't count as a different way) to combine notes within a $\frac{4}{4}$ measure. Also, have students record these combinations symbolically with music notes.

Name _____   Date _____

Chant Reflection

Directions: Answer each question.

1. Write your chant on the lines.

   _____

   _____

   _____

   _____

2. Complete a number sentence for each line of your chant to show how the syllables make one measure:

   _____ = 1

   _____ = 1

   _____ = 1

   _____ = 1

3. What would you say to someone who asked you to explain how to use fractions to represent syllables in a new phrase?

   _____

   _____

   _____

4. Write two new phrases for your chant.

   _____

   _____

#51088—*Strategies to Integrate the Arts in Mathematics*

Poetry

Poetry

Understanding Poetry

Poetry engages students in writing, reading, speaking, and listening. Creating poems can capture the essence of an idea. As stated by Polly Collins, "when students create poems about topics of study, they enhance their comprehension through the connections they have made between the topic and their own lives, the topic and the world around them, and the poetry and the content texts they have read" (2008, 83). Developing mathematical understanding through the creation of poems allows students to consider math concepts in new ways and to share their understanding through language and metaphor. Often, students enjoy creating poems but are not sure how to begin. The strategies in this section provide guidance that will help students identify and work with rich language to explore mathematical ideas. Though poems often rhyme, they do not need to, and sentences don't need to always be complete. "We are more interested in 'surprising images' or words that have a special sound pattern. They empower students to be 'word-gatherers'" (McKim and Steinbergh 1992). Students are invited to put words together in unconventional ways, drawing on evocative language, playful juxtaposition of ideas, and creating images through words as they write poems about concepts in math. This active engagement changes students' relationships with math as they find their own language to describe what they know.

We tend to think about mathematics as working with numbers, and yet theoretical structures of math, vocabulary, and application of math to real-world situations are equally important for students to understand. By working with poetic language, symbolism, and metaphor, students can deepen their understanding of mathematical ideas. As Lipman Bers notes, "mathematics is very much like poetry... what makes a good poem—a great poem—is that there is a large amount of thought expressed in very few words" (quoted in Albers, Alexanderson, and Reid 1990).

Using language to explore mathematical ideas builds conceptual understanding. When your students become poets, they fine-tune their writing and explore the use of patterns, rhythm, and metaphor. Writing poems allows students to use language in fresh ways to develop a deeper understanding of mathematical ideas. As LaBonty and Danielson (2004) note, "it is obvious that both poetry and math rely on patterns and are dependent on students' skill with language, whether it is the language of verse and rhythm or the language of symbols and signs."

Poetry *(cont.)*

Strategies for Poetry

❧ Dialogue Poem

Compare-and-contrast is one of the most effective instructional strategies that teachers can use (Marzano 2007). A dialogue poem encourages students to explore two different perspectives on a topic. This form of poetry works well with opposite but related concepts or perspectives. Similarities and differences between concepts can be explored, giving the rhythm and the feel of a dialogue. The poem is constructed by two writers, encouraging conversation about the content being explored and the ways to best translate ideas into poetic form. This collaborative work allows students to share what they know with their peers and deepen learning. These poems also prompt students to better differentiate between two concepts being learned at the same time.

❧ Rhyme and Rhythm

This strategy invites students to explore and experiment with the sounds of words as they investigate rhythms, asking questions such as, "What patterns feel regular? What patterns change?" Students decide what they like about rhyming and non-rhyming poems. Jan LaBonty notes that "a preference for rhyme and rhythm is contained in the linguistic make-up of all humans; rhyme is easier to recall than prose; rhythm helps carry the predictability of language. There is pattern and measure in every language and in the way we structure our lives" (1997).

Though poems do not need to rhyme, rhymes can unify a poem and the repeated sound can help to connect a concept in one line to that in another. Students create their poems using rhyme and/or rhythms as a way to synthesize learning and distill the essence of concepts and ideas.

Poetry (cont.)

Juxtaposition

This strategy prompts students to find and collect words and phrases from a variety of sources. Students collect and record these words on paper and place them in a "word bowl." Students draw out words and phrases, playing with the juxtaposition of the words. They experiment with line breaks and the creation of meaning in unexpected ways, revealing fresh language and insights into the concepts of study. McKim and Steinbergh note that with word-bowl poetries, "the very fact of manipulating the words, discarding some, trading others, adding what one needs for sense, can teach us something about selection and choice in making poems. Joining two or three words that normally don't appear together can make fresh images, charging them with new energy and excitement" (1992). This strategy allows students to work with descriptions of concepts to create poems that reveal relationships and ideas about content in unique and enlightening language. Putting words together through juxtaposition allows students to boil ideas down to their essence. Students benefit from having a range of words available from which to draw.

Structured Poems

There are many forms of poetry that are created within specified formats. The structure of a certain number of words and syllables or a given pattern of rhythm helps students plan and organize their writing. JoAnne Growney (2009) notes, "Long traditions embrace the fourteen-line sonnet with its ten-syllable lines. Five-line limericks and seventeen-syllable haiku also are familiar forms. Moreover, patterns of accent and rhyme overlay the line and syllable counts for even more intricacy" (12). The possibilities are endless as students engage with different patterns and writing within a particular structure, enabling mathematical concepts to be viewed through a new lens. Furthermore, Corie Herman (2003) suggests that the structured nature of these poems supports diverse students' abilities to succeed in writing them.

Bio Poems

Bio poems often follow a pattern and can be created through student responses to prompts (Kuta 2003). Using the senses to reflect on what has been seen, heard, smelled, touched, and tasted, students become aware of how they (or characters, fictional or real) have been shaped by their unique experiences. This biographical strategy allows students to investigate traditions, attitudes, environmental influences, and commonly held perceptions about a particular idea or within a particular era. The observations and reflections help students become aware of how time and place can influence perspective. When written about themselves, students' bio poems can provide teachers with relevant background information, offer insights on how to best work with individual students, and enhance student–teacher communication.

Dialogue Poems

Model Lesson: Mathematics in Two Voices

Model Lesson Overview

In this strategy, students read a poem written for two voices, brainstorm a list of appropriate mathematical topics for such a poem, and then work individually or in pairs to create their own dialogue poems. As they do so, they gain a deeper understanding of the similarities and differences between two mathematical ideas. These poems also prompt students to better differentiate between two concepts that are learned at the same time and thus differentiate between sometimes confusing factors and multiples.

Standards

K–2

- Counts whole numbers

- Reads a variety of familiar literary passages and texts (e.g., poems)

3–5

- Understands basic number theory concepts (e.g., factors, multiples, divisibility)

- Knows the defining characteristics and structural elements of a variety of literary genres (e.g., poems)

6–8

- Understands the role of negative and positive integers in the number system

- Understands the basic concepts of center and dispersion of data

- Knows the defining features and structural elements of a variety of literary genres (e.g., poems)

9–12

- Understands the properties of the real number system, its subsystems, and complex numbers

- Knows the defining characteristics of a variety of literary forms and genres (e.g., poems)

Materials

- *Examples of Dialogue Poems* (page 150, dialoguepoems.pdf)

- Math texts or related resources

- *Two Voices Poem Plan* (page 151, twovoicesplan.pdf)

Dialogue Poems *(cont.)*

Preparation

Think about mathematical ideas that are related but have different characteristics, such as even and odd numbers, positive and negative numbers, or prime and composite numbers. Brainstorm characteristics of each idea in preparation for a discussion with students.

Familiarize yourself with the two examples of dialogue poems provided in the *Examples of Dialogue Poems* (page 150), or try writing one of your own. Note that each "side" of the poem is to be read by a different voice and the lines in the middle by both voices.

Procedure

1. Display one or all of the dialogue poems in *Examples of Dialogue Poems* (page 150) or share your own creations. Have two students read the different parts of the poem aloud.

2. Ask students, "What do you notice about how these poems are formed? What do you learn about each concept? How does the poem reveal contrasting ideas? What do you notice about the lines read by both voices together?"

3. As a class, brainstorm a list of possible math topics for dialogue poems. Record responses for students to refer to throughout the lesson. See the Specific Grade Level Ideas for additional ideas. Encourage students to use their math textbooks or math literature to draw out more ideas and language that might be incorporated into the poems.

4. Assign or allow students to pick partners and ask them to choose an idea from the brainstormed list that they would like to explore in their dialogue poem. Use the Planning Questions to guide discussion. Distribute *Two Voices Poem Plan* (page 151) to students, and provide time for them to write their dialogue poems. Encourage students to create an image or provide mathematical examples to further exemplify the concepts. If written over time, students can use collaborative technology such as Google Docs™ for their collaboration.

5. Provide students time to practice performing their poems aloud in two voices.

6. Invite students to make audio recordings of their performances and listen and discuss afterward. You can also share these poems on a class blog or by using software that supports voice recording, such as VoiceThread®.

7. Have partners present their poem and image to the rest of the class. Use the Questions for Discussion to debrief.

Dialogue Poems *(cont.)*

Planning Questions

- What words or phrases are associated with each idea?

- What could you write that the voices could read together?

- How will you embed examples of the math within the poem?

- How can you illustrate the poem so that the differences between these concepts are exemplified?

Questions for Discussion

- What differences did you identify between the mathematical concepts?

- What did you learn by writing your poem?

- What might you add to a poem you heard?

- What feedback could you give the teams of authors?

Specific Grade Level Ideas

K–2

Students can draw from a brainstormed list of ideas about differences between the chosen math concepts. You will have greater success if you facilitate the creation of a poem with a small group of learners. Possible topics include addition and subtraction, particular numbers such as one and two, and particular shapes such as triangle and square. Students are likely to focus on examples such as one nose, two eyes, etc.

3–5

Students can work with a partner to write a dialogue poem after a group brainstorming session. In addition to the K–2 Specific Grade Level Ideas, students can consider multiplication and division, factor and multiple, even and odd, area and perimeter, numerator and denominator, and part and whole.

Dialogue Poems *(cont.)*

6–8

In addition to the K–2 and 3–5 Specific Grade Level Ideas, students can consider negative and positive integers, decimal and fraction, rate and ratio, center and variation, and slope and intercept.

9–12

Students can create poems about more advanced properties of the concepts of numbers. Additionally, students can consider independent and dependent variables, linear and quadratic functions, domain and range, surface area and volume, simple and compound interest, and positive and negative correlations.

Examples of Dialogue Poems

Addition and Subtraction

Join

Take away

In all

Left

Combine

Compare

Together

Separate

Sum

Difference

7 plus what
equals 9?

What can I add
to 7 to get 9?

What is 9
minus 7?

Different views of the same thing

Positive and Negative Numbers

Negative numbers

Positive numbers

Less than zero

More than zero

In the red

In the black

Below sea level

Above sea level

Below freezing

Above freezing

Debt

Profit

We balance each
other out

We give symmetry to the number line

Zero is not one of us

Name _____ Date _____

Two Voices Poem Plan

Directions: Use this planning sheet to record the parts of your dialogue poem. Then, on a separate sheet of paper, use this information to create the dialogue poem.

Math Concepts: _____

Poem Title: _____

Voice 1

Terms   Examples

_____   _____

_____   _____

_____   _____

_____   _____

Voice 2

Terms   Examples

_____   _____

_____   _____

_____   _____

_____   _____

Both Voices

_____

_____

_____

_____

_____

_____

Rhyme and Rhythm

Model Lesson: Fact Poems

Model Lesson Overview

Basic-facts fluency is essential to success with mental math and paper-and-pencil strategies with greater numbers. As students create and practice these short poems, they will increase their fact recall and gain insights into fact strategies and properties of arithmetic. Consistent rhyme and rhythm will support student memory, but as students consider meaning and strategies, they should not limit their thinking to specific rhymes or rhyme patterns.

Standards

K–2

- Adds and subtracts whole numbers
- Reads aloud familiar stories, poems, and passages with fluency and expression

3–5

- Multiplies and divides whole numbers
- Understands the ways in which language is used in literary texts (e.g., rhythm)

6–8

- Selects and uses appropriate computational methods for a given situation
- Understands the use of language in literary works to convey mood, images, and meaning (e.g., rhyme, voice, tone, sound)

Materials

- *Example Poems, Grades K–2* (page 156, poemsK–2.pdf)
- *Example Poems, Grades 3–8* (page 157, poems3–8.pdf)
- *Fact Poem Planning Guide* (page 159, factpoemguide.pdf)
- *My Fact Poem* (page 158, factpoem.pdf)

Rhyme and Rhythm *(cont.)*

Preparation

Identify a few short poems that your students will enjoy. Be sure to include one poem that does not rhyme and at least two poems with different rhyme schemes. Plan to make copies of the poems for students. Some poems are suggested in the Specific Grade Level Ideas and are available online. You can also share a math-focused poem such as "One Inch Tall" by Shel Silverstein. Note the rhyme schemes, meter, and rhythmic patterns. For example, "One Inch Tall" has an AABBBC rhyme scheme. For this poem, the number of syllables in each line is also consistent: 14-14-8-8-9-6. This regularity supports memorization.

It is important to focus on the math facts, strategies, and properties that students are beginning to conceptualize or cannot recall quickly. Reflect on your assessment data to identify what you want students to focus on or have students identify the facts they need to memorize or the strategies they want to explore.

Review the sample fact poems provided in *Example Poems, Grades K–2* (page 156) or *Example Poems, Grades 3–8* (page 157). You can share these with students as models, or create examples of your own.

Procedure

1. Read one of the chosen poems aloud to familiarize students with it. As you read the poem, ask students to pay particular attention to the rhyming words and rhythms that they hear.

2. After discussing students' thoughts about the poem, distribute copies of the poem and ask students to note other rhymes or rhythms they identify.

3. Using a second poem, repeat the process so that students recognize that a variety of patterns are possible. Then, repeat with a third poem.

4. Tell students that they can create poems to help them with their math facts. Share the *Example Poems, Grades K–2* (page 156) or the *Example Poems, Grades 3–8* (page 157) with students and tell them that they are going to write their own rhyming fact poems.

5. Assign students fact strategies. Use the Planning Questions to facilitate discussion and planning. Have younger students or students still connecting facts to models complete *My Fact Poem* (page 158). Older students or students focusing on strategies should use the *Fact Poem Planning Guide* (page 159).

6. Once students have created their poems, encourage them to practice reading them with rhythm.

Rhyme and Rhythm (cont.)

7. Have students read their poems aloud. Post the rhymes in the classroom to allow students to refer to them and thus increase the likelihood of understanding and recall.

Planning Questions

• Which fact strategy will you include in your poem?

• What will help you think of rhyming words?

• How might figurative language support your understanding of how a fact strategy works?

• What rhythm will your poem have?

• What image(s) will you use to model your fact poem?

Specific Grade Level Ideas

K–2

"The Drinking Fountain" by Marchette Chute and "The Secret Place" by Tomie dePaola and "April Rain Song" by Langston Hughes are good poems to introduce this activity. Students are likely to find exact rhymes of one-syllable words such as *five* and *hive*. They will be able to recognize words that sound the same but are not spelled the same, such as *eight* and *late*. A standard format of the first line will make it easier for young students to create their own examples. Students just beginning to think about basic facts can create a poem, illustrate it to reinforce the meaning of the addition, and record the related equation on *My Fact Poem*. For students who have an understanding of the concept of addition and are familiar with facts, the poems can serve as a way to develop, recall, or deepen their understanding of fact strategies. Students can create poems for other mathematical concepts such as geometric shapes or units of measurement.

Rhyme and Rhythm *(cont.)*

3–5

"Messy Room" by Shel Silverstein and "Autumn" by Emily Dickinson are good poems to introduce this activity. Introduce the notion of two-syllable rhymes and near- or half-rhymes such as *seven* and *brethren*. These are also called *slant rhymes*. Attention can be given to alliteration and figurative language. Students can create rhymes for multiplication facts and fact strategies as well as other mathematical concepts such as three-dimensional geometric shapes, the rectangular coordinate system, or how to construct or read a graph.

6–8

Introduce the activity with a more sophisticated poem, such as "O Captain! My Captain!" by Walt Whitman. Though students are expected to know their basic facts by this level, there are always some students who do not yet have automaticity and will benefit from this activity. As they experience success, they are likely to recognize the benefits of immediate fact recall. Students can also participate in this work to help younger children learn their facts. Students can create rhymes to help them recall more advanced mathematics concepts such as the order of operations, working with positive and negative integers, statistical data (mean, median, mode), or the defining properties of geometric figures.

Example Poems, Grades K–2

Brother

Ten candies wrapped in silver

Waiting just for me

My brother grabs seven

Now there are only three.

New Books

Went to the library to pick out three

Exciting new books to read.

They were not enough for me,

So back I went for another eight.

$3 + 8 = 11$ stories to read.

They take me to other times and places, it's heaven.

Make a Ten

$5 + 7$ needs to be

$5 + 5 + 2$ for me.

Make a ten, and add two more.

Get to twelve, and get out the door.

Example Poems, Grades 3–8

Rhyme It

Nine times nine is eighty-one.

You know it now. Go have fun.

Distribute It

8 × 3 just needs to be

5 × 3 and 3 × 3.

Add the fifteen to the nine

Twenty-four, and all is fine.

The Doubling Dance

The doubling dance

The doubling dance

Can't leave products up to chance.

2 × 8 is...

16!

Do the doubling dance and find

4 × 8 is...

32!

What can doubling do for you?

Name _____ Date _____

My Fact Poem

Directions: Use the chart to write your math fact poem and illustrate it.

My Math Idea:
My Poem:
My Picture:

Name _____ Date _____

Fact Poem Planning Guide

Directions: Use the chart to brainstorm ideas for your poem.

My topic:
Ideas from images, concepts, facts, and interesting details:
Ideas I would like to incorporate in my poem:
Ideas for rhyming and/or rhythm:

Juxtaposition

Model Lesson: Mathematical Word Bowls

Model Lesson Overview

In this strategy, students brainstorm words they associate with mathematical concepts and put the terms together in new ways to create poems that depict mathematical understanding. Students are encouraged to experiment with a variety of ways to juxtapose the words and may add others as needed.

Standards

K-2

- Uses base-ten concepts to compare whole-number relationships and represent them in flexible ways

- Uses descriptive words to convey basic ideas

3-5

- Understands basic number theory concepts (e.g., factors, multiples, divisibility)

- Uses descriptive and precise language that clarifies and enhances ideas

6-8

- Understands the characteristics and properties of the set of rational numbers and its subsets

- Uses descriptive language that clarifies and enhances ideas

9-12

- Understands the properties of the real number system, its subsystems, and complex numbers

- Uses precise and descriptive language that clarifies and enhances ideas and supports different purposes

Materials

- Reusable containers or shoe boxes

- Chart paper

- Scissors

- *Poetry Word List* (page 164, poetrylist.pdf)

- Microphone (*optional*)

Juxtaposition *(cont.)*

Preparation

At the top of a sheet of chart paper, write mathematical concepts that students are familiar with but about which they need to deepen their understanding. Collect reusable containers or shoe boxes if you wish to have them serve as word bowls. Other ideas are provided in the Specific Grade Level Ideas.

Procedure

1. Have students brainstorm all the words they associate with the chosen concept. Record students' words on chart paper.

2. Cut the chart paper apart so that each word is on a separate piece of paper and place the words in a bowl or other container. Ask students to help you draw several words from the bowl and create a group poem by arranging the selected words. The idea is to put the words together in a variety of ways until they create a clear sense of the idea being explored. As appropriate, encourage metaphors, similes, and the use of imagery, sensory descriptors, and feelings words.

3. After you have completed an example together, students are ready to prepare for their own poems. Divide students into groups of two or three. Assign each group a mathematical concept or allow groups to choose their own. Have groups work with the *Poetry Word List* (page 164), writing words in the spaces provided to build their own lists.

4. Give each group a word bowl (reusable container or shoe box). Have students cut their words apart and place them into the word bowl.

5. Have groups exchange word bowls, making sure that no team receives its original word bowl. Direct students to take 25 words from the bowl and work together to juxtapose them in different ways until they are satisfied with their poem. Tell groups that the selected words are a starting point to spark ideas, so they can exchange words that don't work in the poem or add words they prefer. They can also create phrases, including metaphors and similes, around the words.

6. Once the poems are complete, have students write out a final copy to share with the class. Students can also add images and numbers to illustrate the ideas.

7. Remind students that poems are meant to be heard. Allow group members to rehearse reading their poems aloud to bring them to life.

Juxtaposition *(cont.)*

8. Plan a poetry slam where students present their poems to one another. Bring in a microphone, and invite other classes to hear the poems.

9. Use the Questions for Discussion to debrief the class.

Questions for Discussion

- Why is it important to describe mathematical ideas in words?

- After you brainstormed your ideas, how did you identify the words you selected?

- What did you learn through the process of creating your own poem?

- What unique or fresh language came out of the exploration of juxtaposing different words and phrases?

- What did you learn from listening to the poems of others?

Specific Grade Level Ideas

K–2

Students can work in small groups to brainstorm a smaller number of words. Write student-generated words on slips of paper to add to the word bowl.

Poetry themes can include language related to order and spatial terms and terms such as *tens*, *equal*, and *inches*.

3–5

The activity can be used as written. Possible themes for the poems include fractions, geometric shapes and properties, area, perimeter, and place value.

Juxtaposition *(cont.)*

6–8

After exploring the task as a whole class and giving each group their assigned concept, students can create their initial list of words for homework using the *Poetry Word List*. Then, provide time for students to combine their ideas at the end of the week. Have students provide copies of their first drafts as well as their final poems, along with individual reflections on the process. Students should be expected to produce descriptive language. Possible themes include *slope*, *average*, *intercepts*, *ratios*, and *percent*.

9–12

Adapt this activity according to the 6–8 Specific Grade Level Ideas. Possible themes include *inequality*, *periodicity*, *margin of error*, and *complex numbers*.

Name _____ Date _____

Poetry Word List

Directions: Use the spaces to record and collect words and phrases. Then, cut out the words and place them in your word bowl. Play with the arrangement of the words and phrases to create meaning, mood, and rhythm.

My collection of words and phrases:

Structured Poems

Model Lesson: Cinquain

Model Lesson Overview

The cinquain structure guides the development of a poem by inviting the writer to use a prescribed sequence of words, types of words, or syllables on each line. In this strategy, students write cinquain poems as they note the patterns in the structure and reflect on mathematical concepts and vocabulary.

Standards

K–2

- Counts whole numbers
- Recognizes regularity in a variety of patterns
- Uses descriptive words to convey basic ideas

3–5

- Recognizes a wide variety of patterns and the rules that explain them
- Uses descriptive and precise language that clarifies and enhances ideas

6–8

- Understands various representations of patterns and functions and the relationships among them
- Uses descriptive language that clarifies and enhances ideas

Materials

- *Cinquain Samples* (page 170, cinquainsamples.pdf)
- *Word-Count Cinquain Planner* (page 171, cinquainplanner1.pdf)
- *Parts of Speech Cinquain Planner* (page 172, cinquainplanner2.pdf)
- *Syllable Cinquain Planner* (page 173, cinquainplanner3.pdf)

Structured Poems *(cont.)*

Preparation

Try writing a cinquain poem yourself to experience working within the structure. Reflect on the criteria of the poem that you find easiest to meet and those that you find most challenging. Practice reading cinquains that fit the structure below. See the *Cinquain Samples* (page 170) for examples.

>Line 1: One word—title, noun
>
>Line 2: Two words—adjectives, description or examples
>
>Line 3: Three words—action words (*-ing* words) or further description
>
>Line 4: Four words—feelings or further description
>
>Line 5: One word—synonym of first word or related word

Procedure

1. Display *Cinquain Samples* (page 170), or share your own creation. Read the poems to students, have them read along with you, or ask student volunteers to read the poems. Then, read the poems to students again, asking listeners to keep their eyes closed and visualize what they hear.

2. Ask, "What do you notice about how these poems bring mathematical ideas to life? What do you learn about each concept? How are these poems alike?" Allow time for students to identify ideas related to the number of lines, the number of words in each line, the types of words in each line, the common mathematical theme, and the shape of the poems.

3. Distribute *Word-Count Cinquain Planner* (page 171), *Parts of Speech Cinquain Planner* (page 172), or *Syllable Cinquain Planner* (page 173) to students, whichever is most appropriate for your students.

4. Choose a mathematical topic as a class, and invite students to brainstorm words associated with this topic. Appropriate choices for the first line of the poems are listed in the Specific Grade Level Ideas. You may want to share some of these words with students. You can also refer students to a mathematics word wall, if there's one in your classroom.

5. Once a topic is chosen, brainstorm ideas for the different lines of the poem as a class. Use the Planning Questions to lead discussion. Encourage students to think of examples of the mathematical concept to include a broad range of ways to think about its relationship to real life.

Structured Poems (cont.)

6. Continue as a class, or have students create a cinquain poem in small groups, building on the ideas generated.

7. If appropriate, have students choose their own terms and author their own cinquains. Students may work individually or in pairs.

Planning Questions

- What word will you choose to start your poem? What related word will you use for the last line?

- Close your eyes and think about your word. What do you see? What do you feel? What does this word remind you of? Which words on your list do you like best?

- What actions can you brainstorm that connect to your word? Which action words give new insights about the mathematical ideas?

- What feelings do you associate with this mathematical term?

Specific Grade Level Ideas

K–2

Students can focus on the number of words in each line of a cinquain.

Possible first lines:

- **Counting & Cardinality:** *count*, any number name from one through twenty

- **Operations & Algebraic Thinking:** *addition, difference, equal, equation, sum, subtraction*

- **Number & Operations in Base Ten:** *thousand, hundred, ten*

- **Measurement & Data:** *length, time, ruler, clock, hour, inch, foot, centimeter, meter, minute, graph*

- **Geometry:** *circle, cone, cube, cylinder, hexagon, quadrilateral, rectangle, sphere, square, trapezoid, triangle*

Students can choose a particular number such as the number of children in their family, the number that represents their age, the number of things they wish for (e.g., three new library books to read), or a familiar number (e.g., *one, two,* or *five*).

Structured Poems *(cont.)*

3–5

Students can focus on the number of words in each line or add criteria involving parts of speech or the purpose of the lines. After students write and share their poems, ask students what a decaquain would be (10 lines) and how many total words it would have.

Possible first lines:

- **Operations & Algebraic Thinking:** *array, division, estimation, multiplication, product, equation, quotient, remainder, unknown*

- **Number & Operations in Base Ten:** *digit, million, billion, trillion, decimal, tenths, hundredths, thousandths*

- **Number & Operations—Fractions:** *numerator, denominator, whole*

- **Measurement & Data:** *area, volume, perimeter, degree, kilometer, gram, kilogram, pound, ounce, mass, mile, second, volume, protractor*

- **Geometry:** any name of a shape as well as *angle, endpoint, origin, pentagon, parallel, perpendicular, polygon, point, ray, rhombus, symmetry*

Structured Poems (cont.)

6–8

Students can use the same suggestions as provided in the 3–5 Specific Grade Level Ideas or you can introduce the criteria involving the number of syllables in each line, using the *Syllable Cinquain Planner*.

If the syllabic rules are used, consider challenging students with these questions:

- How many syllables would there be if this were an eight-line structure?

- How many lines would there be if there were a total of 112 words?

- Can you write an equation to predict the number of syllables if you know the number of lines?

Possible first lines:

- **Ratios & Proportional Thinking:** *unit, rate, ratio, percent, proportionality*

- **Expressions & Equations:** *coefficient, equivalent, exponent, inequality, intercept, integer, linear, slope, variable*

- **Geometry:** any name of a shape as well as *circumference, congruence, diameter, dilation, face, edge, net, prism, radius, reflection, rotation, surface area, translation*

- **Statistics & Probability:** *center, chance, distribution, frequency, mean, median, sample, variability*

Cinquain Samples

Two

Hands, feet

Pairing, partnering, doubling

Never one left out

Number

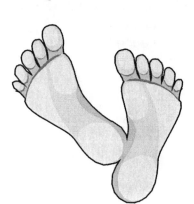

Sphere

Perfectly round

Rolling, spinning, turning

Please throw to me

Ball

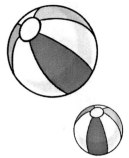

Squares

Four equal sides

Four lines of symmetry

Tessellating across my floor

No holes

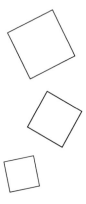

Name _____ Date _____

Word-Count Cinquain Planner

Directions: Collect words and use the planner to create a meaningful cinquain poem.

Mathematical idea for my poem:

_____

_____

_____

Words that describe this idea:

_____

_____

_____

_____

My poem:

Title _____

One word _____

Two words _____ _____

Three words _____ _____ _____

Four words _____ _____ _____ _____

One word _____

Name _____ Date _____

Parts of Speech Cinquain Planner

Directions: Collect words and use the planner to create a meaningful cinquain poem.

Mathematical idea for my poem:

_____

_____

_____

Words that describe this idea:

_____

_____

_____

_____

My poem:

Title _____

Adjectives _____ _____

-ing words _____ _____ _____

Phrase _____ _____ _____ _____

Synonym _____

Name _____ Date _____

Syllable Cinquain Planner

Directions: Collect words and use the planner to create a meaningful cinquain poem.

Mathematical idea for my poem:

_____

_____

_____

Words and phrases that describe this idea:

_____

_____

_____

_____

My poem:

Title _____

Two syllables _____ _____

Four syllables _____ _____ _____ _____

Six syllables _____ _____ _____ _____ _____ _____

Eight syllables _____ _____ _____ _____ _____ _____ _____

Two syllables _____ _____

Bio Poems

Model Lesson: Where I'm from Mathematically

Model Lesson Overview

This particular approach to bio poems is called an "I Am From" poem. "I Am From" poems were developed by teacher and writer George Ella Lyons (2010) and suggest a simple writing prompt for exploring personal histories. An adapted format is used here for exploring mathematical bio poems. Students begin each line with the phrase *I am from* and then introduce specific details of their mathematical histories. The reflective process provides students with the opportunity to find connections among their past experiences, to note how they solve problems and learn best, and perhaps to recognize biases they may bring to the learning of mathematics.

Standards

K–2

- Explains to others how she or he went about solving a numerical problem
- Uses descriptive words to convey basic ideas

3–5

- Understands the general nature and uses of mathematics
- Uses descriptive and precise language that clarifies and enhances ideas

6–8

- Understands the general nature and uses of mathematics
- Uses descriptive language that clarifies and enhances ideas

9–12

- Understands the general nature and uses of mathematics
- Uses precise and descriptive language that clarifies and enhances ideas and supports different purposes

Materials

- *Where I'm from Mathematically Examples* (page 178, wherefrom.pdf)
- *Where I'm from Mathematically Planner* (page 179, wherefromplanner.pdf)

Bio Poems *(cont.)*

Preparation

Read the *Where I'm from Mathematically Examples* (page 178) to become familiar with how the format can be used to write a mathematical autobiography or math-bio poem. You may wish to write a "Where I'm from Mathematically" poem yourself to share with your students. Additional ideas are provided in the Specific Grade Level Ideas.

Procedure

1. Introduce the notion of being "from" someplace. Have students tell how they would respond to someone who asks casually, "Where are you from?" Then, have them discuss what would be different if a good friend asked, "So, how did you get to be you?"

2. Explain to students that they're going to think and write about their mathematical biography or their life story as it relates to math. Read aloud the math-bio poems provided in *Where I'm from Mathematically Examples* (page 178) and have students discuss the ways in which the writers described their mathematical experiences.

3. Distribute the *Where I'm from Mathematically Planner* (page 179) and have students discuss the various categories and some possible responses. For example, in terms of parents, they might think about their parents' attitudes toward math, interests in math, or expectations for learning math. You may wish to review the poems you read in relation to this graphic organizer. Use the Planning Questions to facilitate discussion.

4. After this overview, allow time for students to reflect and record words, phrases, or sentences about their mathematical memories.

5. Have students use their brainstormed words and phrases to create their own "Where I'm from Mathematically" poems. Make sure students understand that they don't have to include all of the topics or all of the words they brainstormed.

6. Provide time for students to edit or critique their poems in pairs. If this is to take place on the following day, encourage students to talk with their families or caregivers about this topic before returning to school. For example, younger students may enjoy learning about how they used to always count when they went up or down stairs. Older students may wish to learn about their parents' mathematical experiences.

Bio Poems *(cont.)*

7. Have students practice presenting their poems orally, providing opportunities to rehearse reading a few times through or with a peer.

8. Have students share and discuss their poems. Use the Questions for Discussion to lead discussion about the poems.

Planning Questions

- Can you tell me more about mathematical moment(s) in your life?

- What are some other words that would help us understand how you felt about math when growing up?

- Was there a teacher who influenced you mathematically? If so, how?

- Are there stories in your life that relate to math?

- Can you include descriptions of mathematical moments in your life that make us feel as if we are there?

- Are there poetic devices you can use (e.g., repetition, metaphor, alliteration)?

Questions for Discussion

- What did you learn about your relationship with math?

- What are some ways our poems are different? The same?

- What do our poems suggest about how we think about mathematics?

- What are some words or phrases that helped us to understand another person's experiences?

- What might cause your poem to change significantly at the end of the year?

Specific Grade Level Ideas

K–2

Students are likely focusing on learning to count. Encourage them to recognize building with blocks and identifying patterns as relevant mathematical experiences. You may wish to have some students work with an adult who can record their thinking. You may be surprised to learn that even these students often have clear views of themselves as learners of mathematics.

Bio Poems *(cont.)*

3–5

Students can interview one another to complete the *Where I'm from Mathematically Planner*. They can imagine that they are reporters trying to get the real story about their classmates' mathematical lives. Memories of learning basic facts may be prominent at this age.

6–8

Students will have several classroom memories. Allow them to describe specific incidents, but ask that they do not mention teachers' names. Encourage these students to probe the thinking of several members of their family and to become sensitive to the ways in which mathematics is portrayed in the media or by teachers of other subjects. Students can take on the persona of a mathematical concept and write a bio poem from that perspective (e.g., "I am a coordinate plane…").

9–12

In addition to the 6–8 Specific Grade Level Ideas, students can write bio poems from the perspective of a career (e.g., "I am an architect…"). To faciliate this, have students imagine life in a particular career, looking back to reflect on the experience. Students may need to conduct research about a particular career to better inform their poems.

Where I'm from Mathematically Examples

I am from a family that works in a store.

They count all day.

"How many paper towels will fit on the shelf?"

I am from sweeping the floor before the big hand is on the six.

I am from "Put the pennies in piles of ten."

I am from number of the day and counting jar.

I am from using fingers and making pictures.

I am from working with my friend Jade.

• •

I am from a father who says, "I don't do math" and a mother who loves to
    solve jigsaw puzzles with a million pieces.

She says, "Try again and again until you find a fit."

I am from playing mystery, card, and strategy games.

The suspect is in the dining room with the rope.

And give me all your twos.

I am from "Solve this problem" and "Tell how you know."

I am from friends who think math is not hot.

I tell them they're wrong and I'll be rich someday.

I am from solving problems by writing equations and making drawings.

I am from using manipulatives and working in groups.

Pattern blocks, tangrams, and geoboards.

I am from feeling proud when I solve a problem that is as hard as stone.

• •

I am from a family who can all do math fast, except for me.

They've got it all figured out before I start.

I am from counting home runs and measuring from scrimmage.

Two downs and four yards to go.

I am from "Let me help you" and "Are you done yet?"

If they left me alone, I could do it myself.

I am from friends who do math as easily as a leaf bends in the breeze.

I am from solving problems by making a guess and working with others.

I am from success if I can work at my own pace.

I am from palms that sweat when I take a test and a heart that beats its
    anxious rhythm.

Name _____ Date _____

Where I'm from Mathematically Planner

Directions: Fill in the boxes to brainstorm ideas for a "Where I'm from Mathematically" poem. Then, on a separate sheet of paper, write your poem, beginning each line with "I am from...."

My family and math:	What I do in my free time and math:
Words or quotes I've heard about math:	My friends and math:
How I solve math problems:	How I learn math best:

#51088—*Strategies to Integrate the Arts in Mathematics*

Storytelling

Storytelling

Understanding Storytelling

Storytelling has been part of every culture since the beginning of time (Norfolk, Stenson, and Williams 2006). Stories have been used to educate, to inspire, and to entertain. There is the story itself, and there is the telling of the tale by a skilled teller. Storytellers use language, gesture, eye contact, tone, and inflection as they share a story with an audience. A good storyteller can create a sense of instant community among listeners as well as a deep connection with the material being explored (Hamilton and Weiss 2005). Because the storyteller interacts with the audience as the story is told, listeners often feel that they become part of the story world. They can even feel as if they were co-creators of the story when it is interactive, when connections with characters are developed, and when empathy is established. If you've ever heard a good storyteller tell a compelling story, you know it can transport you to another time and place.

In the following strategies, students benefit from both listening to stories and from becoming storytellers themselves. As listeners, students are supported in their visualization of the stories, which makes a narrative easier to imagine and remember (Donovan and Pascale 2012). As storytellers, students develop additional skills, including skilled use of voice, improved verbal and nonverbal communication skills, and sense of pacing. Once stories are developed, you can also ask students to write them down, further enhancing their literacy skills.

When your students become storytellers, they fine-tune their communication skills. Oral fluency is developed as students explore vocal tone and inflection, pacing, sound effects, and the addition of rich sensory details to the telling. Listeners feel invited on a journey. Also, participating in the creation and telling of stories brings forth students' voices and their ideas.

Storytelling is not often part of the mathematics classroom (Zazkis and Liljedahl 2009), yet mathematical ideas are easily embedded in or teased out of stories. Students find that stories provide vivid contexts for showing the relevance and use of mathematical thinking. Well-placed mathematical problems can easily be connected to characters' dilemmas, requiring solutions in order for the story to advance. Such dilemmas can provide additional points of interaction for students and heighten the dramatic tension of the story.

As students create, tell, and retell stories, they are gaining fluency in their communication skills, use of descriptive language, and persuasive abilities. They are also expanding their willingness to revisit, revise, and polish their work. By placing mathematics in story settings, we provide a context that gives further meaning to the mathematical ideas and adds interest to the stories.

Storytelling (cont.)

Strategies for Storytelling

☜ Personification

Some people only use *personification* to refer to when we assign human qualities to inanimate objects or ideas, and they use the term *anthropomorphism* when assigning human qualities to animals. Other folks use these terms interchangeably. We will use *personification* to refer to all such assignment of human characteristics as it is most familiar to teachers and students, but feel free to use what best fits your curriculum. Personification is an ancient storytelling tool that continues today; think of both Aesop and the Toy Story movies (Cahill 2006). Stories that give animals and objects human traits allow listeners to think about their shortcomings in a safe way and invite us to think about moral or ethical values. These tales engage learners and allow us to consider different perspectives. Because animals and objects take on human characteristics, the strategy also lends itself to figurative language.

☜ Prompt

Students are invited to become storytellers themselves as they brainstorm, develop, and perform stories from a given prompt. In this strategy, we use prompts as story starters. Students are given both a scenario and a visual cue to be woven into their stories. Students are charged with finding a way for the story to unfold and are in control of its progression. This strategy works to develop many skills—understanding of beginning, middle, and end; character development; and the significance of circumstance, setting, and mood in creating compelling stories that are performed and engage the listener.

In language arts, students might be given a story starter such as, "It was cold and damp and the wind was fierce, but I had to go out to save my friend." Students then continue the story, using their imaginations to build the tale. In mathematics, we usually provide students with a word problem without allowing them to elaborate on it by adding details that would make the stories more interesting. Occasionally, we present an equation and ask students to create a word problem to match it. The result is usually standard stories that mimic those found in textbooks. According to Gadanidis, Gadanidis, and Huang, the good mathematics story offers students the incentive to give their attention and the opportunity to gain mathematical insight (2005).

Storytelling (cont.)

Exaggeration

It's human nature to exaggerate to make our stories more interesting. Often, we hear someone's story and have the desire to top it with something bigger, better, or more grandiose from our own treasure trove of experiences. Storytellers use exaggeration to emphasize their points and to pique the interest of their audiences. In fact, storyteller Jim Green identifies hyperbole as a tool in the storyteller's toolbox (Wohlberg 2012).

In this strategy, exaggeration can be enhanced by the inclusion of intentionally false mathematical information, providing a vehicle for further developing students' sense of numbers and measures. As in other techniques, embedding math concepts in a story allows students to experience a context in which math knowledge is useful.

The Untold Story

In this strategy, students are asked to consider the fact that every story is told from a particular perspective. In foregrounding one vantage point, the viewpoints of others are minimized, marginalized, or even left out. Perspective taking is critical to students' social development, and "understanding the perspective of others is an important skill that benefits children in their complex reasoning abilities that are important in math problems, such as story problems" (Heagle and Rehfeldt 2006, 32). This strategy asks students to consider whose perspective is prominent in a story and what voices or concepts are missing. Inviting students to begin looking for missing voices or ideas can develop critical thinking skills and empathy.

Points of Entry

Entering at different points of the story can provide different structures for building a narrative. We have prequels that start before stories, we can add a new segment to the middle of a story, and in daily life, we sometimes work backward to figure out where we need to begin. These different points of entry provide a frame that can support students' abilities to create a story as well as to gain a deeper understanding of cause-and-effect relationships. In creating such stories, students analyze, evaluate, and create, the three highest-order thinking skills in Benjamin Bloom's revised taxonomy (Anderson et al. 2000).

Personification

Model Lesson: Trickster Tales

Model Lesson Overview

Fables and trickster tales are short narratives that often involve animal characters with human traits. In this strategy, a trickster tale about a fox is explored as students consider the ways in which he trades coins with other animals. Students consider the trades, keeping track of the money the trickster gains. As these stories often focus on what is right and wrong and the trickster makes convincing arguments, they provide excellent vehicles for exploring ideas of equivalence.

Standards

K–2

- Adds and subtracts whole numbers
- Improvises dialogue to tell stories

3–5

- Knows approximate size of basic standard units and relationships between them
- Improvises dialogue to tell stories

6–8

- Solves problems involving units of measurement and converts answers to a larger or smaller unit within the same system
- Creates characters, environments, and actions that create tension and suspense

9–12

- Understands the properties of the real number system, its subsystems, and complex numbers
- Constructs imaginative scripts that convey story and meaning to an audience

Materials

- *Fox at the Carnival* (pages 191–192, foxcarnival.pdf)
- Real or play money
- *Character Development Planner* (page 193, character.pdf)
- *Math Plot Planner* (page 194, plot.pdf)

Personification (cont.)

Preparation

Read through *Fox at the Carnival* (pages 191–192) and think about how you will tell it. Think about how you want to establish the sense of setting so that students can imagine where the story unfolds. Decide on the voices you will use so that each character is distinct. Note ways to bring the story to life through animated storytelling. When telling *Fox at the Carnival* to your students, breathe deeply to smell the popcorn, pant like the dog, stand on your tiptoes as the gopher looks out, and make a fantastic hissing sound. Feel free to add your own language and sensory details while telling the story to make it come to life. Engage your listeners by using pauses, eye contact, and movement to hold attention and to create suspense. Imagine that you were witness to the story as it unfolded and are sharing it with them with a sense of urgency and excitement. As you tell the story, you can create interactive moments through whispered asides, such as, "How much do three nickels make?" and wait for audience helpers to respond. Invite students into the story by asking, "Do you smell the popcorn?" Encourage everyone to act as if they were smelling deeply. Ask, "What else do you notice? Ah yes, the bright lights of the rides illuminate the sky."

Modeling the story with money will engage students in the tricks. Gather real or play money to use in your telling of the story. Other ideas are provided in the Specific Grade Level Ideas.

Procedure

1. Announce that you have a trickster tale to share, and tell the story without the math calculations.

2. Tell students that you want to tell the story again and have them become the animals to help bring the story to life. Ask them to come up with gestures to depict different animals, such as the gopher on its toes, the dog with its tongue hanging out, and the slithering snake. Practice the gestures and divide students into animal groups. During your retelling of the story (without the math calculations), encourage students to add sounds and movement when their character is introduced.

3. Create gestures and sounds that help establish the setting. Ask students how they can show the smell of the popcorn, the jostling crowd, the bright lights, and the whirling rides with gestures and sounds. Have students share their suggestions for these aspects of the setting and select students to practice them. Retell the story (without the math calculations), and have students supply the animal sounds and movements as well as the setting sounds and gestures.

4. Tell students that you will need them to help calculate the math so that you can all see the trick that's being played. Provide real or play money and retell the story again, this time pausing for students to model the scenes and calculate the amounts.

Personification *(cont.)*

5. After each exchange, discuss the relationship between the two collections or items as you guide with questions such as, "How much do three nickels make?" Ask student volunteers to record the amount on paper, and then ask them to arrange their arms to represent the > or < relationship or have them record the related equations.

6. Ask students to identify character traits that can be associated with a trickster (e.g., *sly, slinky, greedy, untrustworthy*) and what gestures could be used to suggest these traits (e.g., slinking, reaching out, looking over his shoulder constantly).

7. Distribute the *Character Development Planner* (page 193) and the *Math Plot Planner* (page 194), and have small groups of students use them to create their own trickster tales.

8. As students work together, use the Planning Questions to guide their thinking. Provide time for groups to dramatize their stories as one group member narrates. Students in the audience should record the mathematical representation each time the trickster plays his or her tricks.

Planning Questions

- Where will your story unfold? What will you see, smell, hear, and touch in this location?

- What will be your character's traits? How will they sound? What props and gestures can you use to develop each character and demonstrate his or her traits?

- Why does the trickster want money? How much money does he or she have now? What tricks will be played? How much money will the trickster have then?

Storytelling

Personification (cont.)

Specific Grade Level Ideas

K–2

The story can be used as written for second-grade students. Have kindergarten and first-grade students create a story involving counting such as, "Your five pennies are so dull," said Fox. "I have shiny pennies, so I will give you these five shiny ones for your five dull ones." The narrator portrays Fox counting from one to five but touching one penny twice, giving only four coins away.

Students can use addition and number sense in their stories. For example, "I see you have a group of two pennies and a group of seven pennies," said Fox. "Two pennies is so little, I will give you a group of four pennies and another group of four pennies."

3–5

Increase the number of coins in the collections. Students can compare the values of fractions. For example, "You only have $\frac{1}{2}$ of a pie. I will give you $\frac{4}{10}$ of a pie. Four and ten are greater numbers than one and two." The stories can also involve multiplication. Use the story as written (changing collections as students' skills evolve), and have them use multiplication equations to find the total values.

Have fifth-grade students find the differences between the collections of coins by using decimal notation. Include comparison of measurement. For example, "I see you have two pounds of gold," said Fox. "Two is so little and I have lots of gold. I will trade you my 24 individual ounces of gold for your two pounds."

© *Shell Education*   #51088—*Strategies to Integrate the Arts in Mathematics*   **189**

Personification *(cont.)*

6–8

Students can use the 3–5 Specific Grade Level Ideas by increasing or decreasing the size of the numbers. Have students include decimals in measurement comparisons. For example, "I see you have 123.6 cm of beautiful ribbon," said Fox. "Centimeters are so short, and I have lots of ribbon. I will trade you my piece of ribbon that is 1.22 m long."

Students can include examples that involve comparison of expressions and faulty applications of the order of operations or the distributive property. For example, "Look at these eight shiny quarters. I will give you double the number of these quarters for all of your ride tickets. Oh, but I do want to keep two of the quarters for sentimental reasons." The narrator then portrays Fox taking away two quarters first before doubling the number, rather than doubling first and then taking two away.

9–12

Additional tricks include making the slope negative, increasing intercept while decreasing slope and extending the period of time, or including an error when distributing a negative sign with absolute value.

Fox at the Carnival

(Bold words indicate interactive moments.)

One night, Fox was wandering down the road to one of his favorite places, the carnival. He loved the **smell of the popcorn**, the **feel of the jostling crowd**, and the sight of the **bright lights** illuminating the sky as the **rides whirled in circles**. The only problem was that he only had three nickels, and he knew that fifteen cents was not enough.

He was busy thinking about how he could get some more money when he saw Dog sitting by the trail. As usual, **Dog's tongue hung out of his mouth as he panted noisily**. Fox asked Dog if he was going to the carnival, and Dog proudly showed Fox his three dimes.

"Those coins are so small," said Fox. "I am rich, so I will give you these three really big nickels for your three small dimes."

"Wow!" exclaimed Dog as he made the trade. "Thank you, Fox. See you at the carnival."

Calculate!

How many cents are three nickels worth? *(15 cents)*

How many cents are three dimes worth? *(30 cents)*

How can we write this comparison mathematically? *(15 < 30)*

How much money has Fox gained? *(15 cents)*

What equation can we write to show this? *(30 – 15 = 15)*

Fox was grinning about his thirty cents when he saw **Gopher standing high on her toes, looking out of her hole**. Fox asked Gopher if she was going to the carnival, and Gopher proudly showed Fox her two quarters.

"You only have two coins," said Fox. "I am rich, so I will give you these three dimes for your two quarters."

"Wow!" exclaimed Gopher as she made the trade. "Thank you, Fox. See you at the carnival."

Fox at the Carnival (cont.)

Calculate!

How many cents are three dimes worth? *(30 cents)*

How many cents are two quarters worth? *(50 cents)*

How can we write this comparison mathematically? *(30 < 50)*

How much money has Fox gained? *(20 cents)*

What equation can we write to show this? *(50 – 30 = 20)*

Fox was grinning about his fifty cents when he saw **Spider weaving his silky web**. Fox asked Spider if he was going to the carnival, and Spider proudly showed Fox his one dollar bill.

"You only have paper money that can rip or burn," said Fox. "I am rich, so I will give you these two silver quarters for your dollar."

Wow!" exclaimed Spider as he made the trade. "Thank you, Fox. See you at the carnival."

Calculate!

How many cents is a dollar worth? *(100 cents)*

How many cents are two quarters worth? *(50 cents)*

How can we write this comparison mathematically? *(100 > 50)*

How much money has Fox gained? *(50 cents)*

What equation can we write to show this? *(100 – 50 = 50)*

Fox was grinning about his dollar when he saw **Snake slithering among the tall grass** where she had heard what Fox had been doing. Fox asked Snake if she was going to the carnival. Snake lifted her head and made a loud hissing noise. So much air came out of Snake's mouth that it blew Fox's dollar far, far away, where Dog, Gopher, and Spider found it.

"See you at the carnival," said Snake, and she slithered back into the grass.

Name _____ Date _____

Character Development Planner

Directions: Use this chart to develop ideas for the animals your trickster will meet.

Animal 1	Animal 2	Animal 3
Character Traits	Character Traits	Character Traits
Voice	Voice	Voice
Props	Props	Props
Gestures	Gestures	Gestures

Name _____   Date _____

Math Plot Planner

Directions: Use this chart to help you plan your mathematical trickster tale.

Who is your trickster? _____

What does your trickster have? _____

Why does your trickster want more? _____

_____

Trickster has:	Trickster has:	Trickster has:
First animal has:	Second animal has:	Third animal has:
Mathematical representation of the comparison:	Mathematical representation of the comparison:	Mathematical representation of the comparison:
Trickster's trick:	Trickster's trick:	Trickster's trick:
Trickster gained:	Trickster gained:	Trickster gained:
Mathematical equation:	Mathematical equation:	Mathematical equation:

At the end of the story, how does your trickster lose what he or she has gained?

_____

_____

_____

Prompt

Model Lesson: Story Starters

Model Lesson Overview

These story starters provide a combination of mathematical prompts (pictures, graphs, and equations) along with an introductory scenario to trigger students' thinking about a mathematical story they could tell. Students work in groups to create their own stories, increasing the likelihood that they will participate in mathematical conversations and better understand the relevance of mathematics to their lives.

Standards

K–2

- Uses discussions with teachers and other students to understand problems
- Writes or records dialogue

3–5

- Uses a variety of strategies to understand problem situations
- Writes or records dialogue

6–8

- Formulates a problem, determines information required to solve the problem, chooses methods for obtaining this information, and sets limits for acceptable solutions
- Refines and records dialogue and action

Materials

- *Story Starter Cards* (pages 198–200, startercards.pdf)
- *Story Starter Organizer* (pages 201–202, storyorganizer.pdf)

Preparation

Examine the story starter examples given in the Specific Grade Level Ideas. Reproduce the appropriate cards from *Story Starter Cards* (pages 198–200) to display for students. If you wish to adapt these prompts or create your own, you will need to create or find a visual prompt that will generate curiosity and provide a catalyst for each story. This could be a bar graph, a line graph, or an image that will prompt mathematical thinking.

Prompt (cont.)

Decide how you want to use grouping for this activity. Do you want individual students to think of their own stories to bring to their groups to consider? Do you want students to brainstorm with a group right from the beginning? Do you want groups of students to create a story from the same starter, or do you want some groups to have different beginnings?

Plan working groups so that each group consists of students with a variety of abilities. Students with strengths in telling stories, creating stories, and thinking mathematically can all bring their unique capabilities to the task.

Procedure

1. If your students are not familiar with what a story starter is, explain the concept.

2. Share your chosen story starter card (*Story Starter Cards*, pages 198–200) with students. Read the story starter aloud and ask questions to help students think about what might happen next and to identify a potential conflict in the story.

3. Draw students' attention to the visual prompt and ask them to identify what it tells them and how it might relate to the story.

4. In small groups, have students brainstorm ways to connect the starting scenarios with the visual prompt and decide what conflict could arise in the story and how the conflict could be resolved. Use the Planning Questions to guide students' thinking.

5. Have students share their ideas with the class.

6. Tell each group to choose one of the ideas and develop it further. Distribute the *Story Starter Organizer* (pages 201–202) and have students use the organizer to record their thinking.

7. Provide time for students to develop and practice telling their stories and then present them out loud. Encourage students to develop ways to differentiate their characters with different voices, to invite interactive moments for listeners, and to use gestures and expression to bring the story to life.

8. Have students identify the different ways in which mathematics was integrated into the stories.

Prompt *(cont.)*

Planning Questions

- What does this visual prompt or story idea tell you? When do you use this type of mathematics? Are there other ways to represent these mathematical ideas? What characters are suggested? Events?

- How will you integrate this mathematical information into your story? Will it be connected to the conflict or the resolution in the story? What mathematical dilemma might your characters encounter?

- What other related mathematical ideas can you include in this story? How might the progression of events in your story build interest, come to a climax, and end in a resolution?

- How might you engage with your audience as you tell the story?

Specific Grade Level Ideas

K–2

Have students work with you or another adult in the classroom. You can include the mathematical expressions provided, depending on your students' needs and abilities.

3–5

As an extension, have students build on others' ideas. For example, one group can offer a few sentences to begin the story, ending with "and then," which signals the next group to continue from this point.

6–8

Students can have a competition to see which group can come up with the most creative story with the greatest number of mathematical ideas. As an extension, make two spinners, one with random equations, such as $4x + 217 = 281$, and one with random settings, such as *health club* or *sports stadium*. Students spin both spinners and then combine the two results to tell a story.

Story Starter Cards

K–2

It was a bright, sunny day for my birthday party. I was just about to give each friend a cupcake when there was a loud noise behind me.

$$12 - 7$$

Our class had a field day yesterday with lots of contests. The tug-of-war contest was really funny.

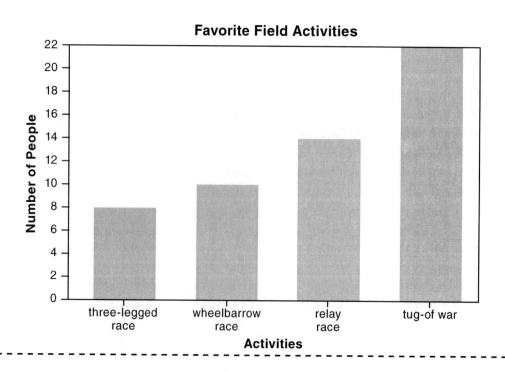

Story Starter Cards *(cont.)*

3–5

I've always been afraid of dogs, but I need $100 and I need it now.

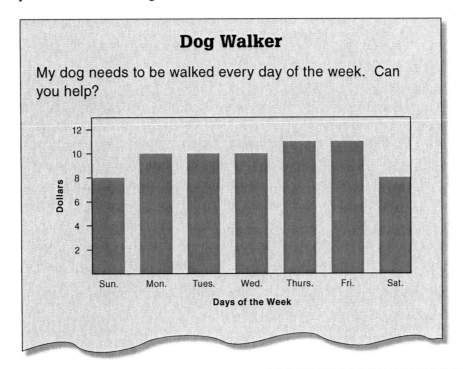

Dog Walker

My dog needs to be walked every day of the week. Can you help?

It was going to be the best scavenger hunt ever. I really wanted the teams to be even so that everyone would have a great time, but it didn't work out that way in the beginning.

Scavenger Hunt List

1. a raw egg signed by a police officer

2. a menu from a restaurant

3. a quarter from 1994

24 people ÷ 5 = 4 r4

Story Starter Cards (cont.)

6–8

My name is Chris, and I am a champion skateboarder. Yesterday I was boarding along when something very strange happened.

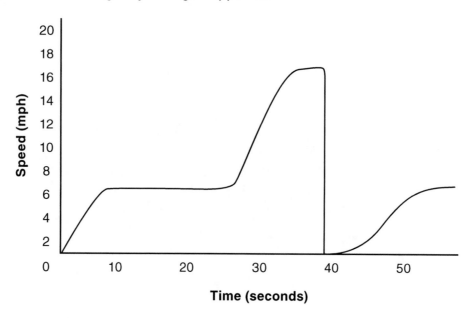

Finally, my mother said I could have a cell phone. She decided this because yesterday it would have really made a difference if I owned a phone.

Choosing a Plan

Individual Plans

- Unlimited nationwide calling

- Unlimited domestic messages

- No annual contract!

Family Plans

- Unlimited calls and messages nationwide

- Two-line minimum to get started

- 1 year contract

Story Starter Organizer

Directions: Use the questions to help you write your story.

1. What is the first sentence of the story?

   _____

   _____

2. What are two important things that will happen in your story?

   _____

   _____

3. What are three math ideas that you will include in your story?

Name _____ Date _____

Story Starter Organizer *(cont.)*

4. What creative choices will you use to tell the story (use of voice, gesture, and interactive moments)?

_____

_____

_____

_____

_____

5. How will the story end?

_____

_____

_____

_____

_____

_____

_____

_____

Exaggeration

Model Lesson: Tall Tales

Model Lesson Overview

Tall tales are filled with exaggerations. In America, these tales are part of American folk legend and are associated with the Wild West. The tales often begin with the character's childhood and are filled with impossible feats. Good number and measurement sense include the ability to recognize when numbers or measurements just don't seem right. In this strategy, students create exaggerated statements that involve measurements or numbers, recognize mathematically related exaggerations in a tall tale that is read to them, and create their own tall tales.

Standards

K-2

- Makes quantitative estimates of familiar linear dimensions, weights, and time intervals and checks them against measurements

- Plans and records improvisations based on personal experience and heritage, imagination, literature, and history

3-5

- Uses specific strategies to estimate quantities and measurements

- Plans and records improvisations based on personal experience and heritage, imagination, literature, and history

6-8

- Selects and uses appropriate estimation techniques to solve real-world problems

- Creates improvisations and scripted scenes based on personal experience and heritage, imagination, literature, and history

Materials

- Exaggerated measurement statements

- *Tall Math Sentences* (page 208, tallmath.pdf)

- *Tall Tale Organizer* (page 209, talltale.pdf)

Exaggeration *(cont.)*

Preparation

To help get students thinking about exaggeration, create exaggerated measurement statements for them to top such as, "I was so tired that I slept for two years, and when I woke up, I didn't fit into any of my clothes." You can use the prompts in *Tall Math Sentences* (page 208) for ideas.

Tall tales are associated with the legend of the American frontier, so select a tale or a section of a tall tale to tell to your students. Practice telling the story aloud, and use your voice to make the story even more interesting. Think about exaggerations related to number or measurements that you can highlight. For example, Paul Bunyan is said to have dug Lake Michigan to create a watering hole for his ox, Babe, and to have had a kitchen that was 10 miles long. What gestures might you use to emphasize these large measures? How might you engage your students in participating in the story? There may be moments when they join in by speaking choral lines or perform gestures to indicate the entrance or actions of a character.

Tall tales were often told aboard steamships or around campfires. Think about ways to create such an atmosphere in your classroom by sitting in a circle and turning off the lights. In choosing the tale to tell, consider how marginalized groups are depicted and how to address this with students. You may choose to edit such text or point out the negative depictions as examples of prejudice and discuss how the story could be adjusted to be more inclusive and equitable. Other ideas are provided in the Specific Grade Level Ideas.

Procedure

1. Share the exaggerated measurement statements you created and ask students to top your tales by creating even greater exaggerations.

2. Once students have been sensitized to exaggerations of measure, tell a tall tale or a section of a tall tale and ask students to describe features of the story. Tell students that the tale was written a long time ago when people were pioneers moving to the West. Ask students to brainstorm why exaggeration might be important at such a time or, if more appropriate to the group, times when they hear or use exaggeration.

3. Explain that you are going to retell the story, but that this time, whenever there's a statement about numbers or measurements that has been exaggerated, you want students to raise their hands. Note that students will need to estimate to note these exaggerations. Retell the tall tale, and have students signal when they hear the misinformation.

Exaggeration (cont.)

4. Provide prompts for students to complete and build on, using exaggerated numerical or measurement data. For example:

- I was _____ long when I was born. I was so long that _____.

- (Name) has _____ books. (He/She) has so many books that (he/she) could _____.

- (Name) ran at a speed of _____. At that speed, (he/she) could _____.

5. Have students complete the prompts with a partner and then share them with the class. If you want students to create more exaggerated sentences, distribute *Tall Math Sentences* (page 208), and have students complete the prompts provided.

6. Have students work individually, in pairs, or in triads to create their own tall tales. Remind them to think about their main character's traits and the problem he or she will face, and to make mathematical exaggerations part of the story. Distribute the *Tall Tale Organizer* (page 209) and have students use it to plan for their stories. Use the Planning Questions to guide students' thinking.

7. Allow time for students to practice telling their stories. Remind them about the importance of voice and gesture in the development of characters. Ask students to consider how they will portray different characters and how they will move between the roles of narrator and characters. How will they match the exaggeration in the stories with artistic choices in their storytelling technique (voice, gesture, facial expression, etc.)?

8. Have students share their work in a "Tall Tales Marathon."

Planning Questions

Measurement:

- What measurement do you want to exaggerate?

- What would be a really small or really large measurement using this unit?

- Why is this measurement important to the character, setting, or plot?

- What would be humorous about this exaggerated measurement?

Numbers:

- What numerical data do you want to exaggerate?

- What will these numbers tell us about the character?

- How might these numbers be related to solving the problem in the story?

Exaggeration *(cont.)*

Storytelling:

- How will you establish a sense of character by using voice, gesture, and facial expression?

- How will you engage your audience?

- How might voice and gesture be used to emphasize the exaggerations in your story?

- When might your character speak? How will your voice change to indicate a new speaker?

Story elements:

- How will your story begin?

- What problem will your character face?

- What parts of your story will be told by a narrator?

Specific Grade Level Ideas

K–2

Focus on tall sentences rather than tall tales for most students at this level. Refer to the prompts provided in *Tall Math Sentences.*

Young students are familiar with names of large numbers even if they don't understand the place-value concepts related to such numbers. Some students will add many zeros to a number, and others may create a number name such as *gazillion millions.* Encourage students to follow their own intuitions as they build a deeper understanding that numbers are infinite.

Length, time, and money are the focus of measurement at this level. Students will also benefit from the opportunity to use comparative terms such as *shortest, tallest, widest,* and *longest.*

Exaggeration *(cont.)*

3–5

As well as with length, time, and money, students can work with liquid measurements, mass, area, and perimeter. To challenge students, have them identify types of measurements they should include in their stories.

Introduce the term *hyperbole*, and have students become mathematical hyperbole detectives. For example, "My brother said he had tons of homework to do." Designate an area where "findings" can be displayed.

6–8

Students can create a tall tale about a sports or pop star or imagine themselves as the central character in the story.

Have students explore the rates of exaggeration in existing tales or in those they create to determine if the rates are proportional. For example, if a male adult character is 60 feet tall, is his chair 10 times the usual size as well?

Have students include exaggerations related to angle measures, volume, and surface area. One student included the following in her tall tale about a super-detective: "My peripheral vision is so powerful that I can see as wide as 3,600 degrees. In fact, sometimes my eyes spin around so many times that robbers get dizzy looking at me and fall to the ground."

Name _____ Date _____

Tall Math Sentences

Directions: Add interesting words and phrases to create exaggerated sentences. Make your tales as tall as possible! Then, write your own "Tall Sentence."

1. My foot is _____ long. It is so long that _____

   _____

   _____

   _____.

2. It takes me _____ to walk to school. I walk so fast that _____

   _____

   _____

   _____.

3. My pockets are full of money. I have _____ . That is enough money to

   _____

   _____

   _____.

Write your own "Tall Sentence."

_____

_____

_____

_____

_____

Name _____ Date _____

Tall Tale Organizer

Directions: Use the questions to help you write your tall tale.

1. My character's name is _____.

2. The problem that my character needs to solve is _____.

3. The three character traits that will help to solve the problem are _____, _____, and _____.

4. List mathematical exaggerations for each trait. Be sure to include exaggerations involving numbers and measurements.

Trait #1

Trait #2

Trait #3

The Untold Story

Model Lesson: Math Sidebars

Model Lesson Overview

There are numerous stories that have been purposely written to combine mathematics and literature, but what about those stories that do not highlight mathematical ideas? In this strategy, students consider mathematical information that may be missing from stories and add it in as a sidebar. A sidebar can be thought of as a story within a story. It is often boxed off and provides details about a related part of a story. Students create math sidebars that share the relevant mathematics embedded in a story, though perhaps hidden from view, and alert listeners to the pervasive nature of mathematics.

Standards

K–2

- Understands that numerals are symbols used to represent quantities or attributes of real-world objects

- Plans and records improvisations based on personal experience and heritage, imagination, literature, and history

3–5

- Understands that numbers and the operations performed on them can be used to describe things in the real world and predict what might occur

- Plans and records improvisations based on personal experience and heritage, imagination, literature, and history

6–8

- Understands the general nature and uses of mathematics

- Creates improvisations and scripted scenes based on personal experience and heritage, imagination, literature, and history

9–12

- Understands the general nature and uses of mathematics

- Improvises, writes, and refines scripts based on personal experience and heritage, imagination, literature, and history

Materials

- Book containing sidebars

- *What's Been Untold?* (page 216, untold.pdf)

The Untold Story *(cont.)*

Preparation

Read the Procedure and rehearse telling the well-known story of *Hansel and Gretel*. Determine what voice to use for these mathematical sidebars. For example, do you want to use the voice of young Hansel or the authoritative voice of a mathematical expert?

Find an example of a book with sidebars to share with students.

Identify stories familiar to students and brainstorm mathematical questions they could ask related to the characters, plots, or settings. Read the Specific Grade Level Ideas, and identify ones that would work well with books or historical contexts appropriate for your students.

Procedure

1. Introduce the idea of a sidebar by showing students a book with sidebars and ask students to share any familiarity they have with the use of sidebars in a story.

2. Explain to students that some important facts about the story of *Hansel and Gretel* have been untold but that these facts are now going to be included in mathematical sidebars. Retell the story of *Hansel and Gretel*, stopping after Hansel marks the path with white pebbles from his pocket. Say to students, "And here is the first part of the story that's untold. Hansel had to think carefully about how many pebbles would fit into his pocket and when to place one on the ground. His thinking went like this: "I know I only have 15 pebbles to use. If I place one here, when should I put the next one down? Should I place one every 50 feet, every 100 steps, or even farther apart? How will I decide?"

3. Provide time for students to talk about the problem Hansel faced and how mathematics could help him. What investigations could they carry out to help them decide what Hansel should do?

4. Return to the story and stop again when Hansel uses bread crumbs to mark the trail. You may wish to again provide the related mathematical sidebar or invite a student to do so. The sidebar may be similar to the one about the pebbles, but the bread crumbs also suggest a question of size. How small can the crumbs be and still be effective? You may invite students to consider that animals ate every other bread crumb, leaving more distance between each crumb.

The Untold Story (cont.)

5. Finally, elaborate through a mathematical sidebar Hansel's placement in the cage, mentioning the probable size of the cage as compared to Hansel's height. Have students discuss how these mathematical ideas help listeners to better understand Hansel's thinking and what happened to him. As a class, summarize these ideas by completing *What's Been Untold?* (page 216) using the story of *Hansel and Gretel* as a model.

6. Divide students into groups and assign them a story they know or a historical period to capture within a story, or allow them to choose a story of their own. Have them brainstorm possible untold mathematical components in their assigned story. Distribute *What's Been Untold?* and have students complete it as they brainstorm their sidebars. Use the Planning Questions to guide students' thinking.

7. Allow time for groups to practice telling the story (or sections of the story) with the mathematical sidebars included.

8. Have groups share their stories, engaging their listeners in solving the mathematical dilemmas. Use the Questions for Discussion to debrief with students.

Planning Questions

- From whose or what perspective will you tell the story? How will this influence how you tell the story?

- What numbers could you use to tell about the story setting?

- When will you stop the story to tell the untold mathematical sidebar?

- How will you show the shift between the narrator and the character(s) so that the audience knows who is speaking?

Questions for Discussion

- What did you discover about how math functions in stories?

- Why did the character in the story need to use math?

- How can math add new details to a story?

The Untold Story (cont.)

Specific Grade Level Ideas

All students can benefit from exploring *Hansel and Gretel* as an introductory example. Ideally, this mathematical lens is applied frequently so that it becomes a classroom norm to ask, "How can mathematics help me to better understand a story? Character choices? Story events? This setting? This dilemma?" Search within the story for mathematical moments that will allow students to identify and tell an "untold story."

K–2

Using familiar stories, work with students as a class to create mathematical sidebars. Many fairy tales lend themselves to mathematical analysis. *Goldilocks and the Three Bears* is a well-known favorite. Students can further investigate the length of a bed that would be too small or too big for students in the class. Focusing on the moment when Goldilocks discovers the sizes of different beds, create a sidebar in which Goldilocks, for example, takes out measuring tape she always carries—just in case—and measures the beds against her four-foot length. Students can tell richly detailed descriptions of this moment in the story, or they can add in her discovery of another "too big, "too small," or "just right" comparison.

Students relate easily to *Alexander and the Terrible, Horrible, No Good, Very Bad Day* by Judith Viorst. Younger students can simply count all of the horrible things that happen to Alexander in one day and retell the story, referring to the events by number. They can tell a story about another day in Alexander's life that was not shared in the book and elaborate on the details and numbers of events that occur in this untold story. Older students can retell the story using a clock to show the estimated times at which these events occurred. As a follow-up activity, students can create their own horrible-day stories in which at least three numbers are used.

The Untold Story (cont.)

3–5

A Chair for My Mother by Vera Williams is about family members who save coins in a jar so that they can buy a chair. The focus on money can lead to many questions about savings, the possible size of the jar, and the possible value of the coins.

Have students read a book connected to the westward expansion of the United States such as *Dandelions* by Eve Bunting. Students can explore questions such as, "How much food should a family bring for such a trip? How much space would there be in the wagon for these provisions? How many miles per day would the family have to walk to make the trip?" Students can add parallel stories from their lives that mirror the ideas in the story but draw out their own real-life examples.

There are a variety of books written about emigrants. Quantitative data and relationships can help us to better understand cultural differences. Encourage students to retell such a story but to do so with mathematical sidebars. A co-storyteller weaves in mathematical information that compares populations, temperatures, currency, and so forth of the original and current homeland.

6–8

Have students read a book about the Great Depression such as *The Mighty Miss Malone* by Christopher Curtis. Any number of scenes can be considered, or you can have students investigate the financial hardships of this time period as compared to those experienced today.

Applying a mathematical lens to a biography of a sports star can further amplify the magnitude of that person's success and the life of an athlete. For example, "How many calories did Michael Phelps need to eat each day when he was in training? What would you eat to get that many calories? If Carl Lewis could maintain his greatest speed for one hour, how far could he run? How could you estimate the number of miles Wilma Rudolph ran in her lifetime? What percentage of athletes who compete in the Olympics win a medal?" Have students include five key mathematical facts as they tell the story of a sports star's life with rich details that bring the story to life.

Hold an Untold Story contest. Students only tell the mathematical sidebars and contestants compete to identify the matching story.

The Untold Story *(cont.)*

9–12

Have students make connections to topics covered in their history textbooks by considering which math sidebars would help them to better understand the time period. For example, students studying the Revolutionary War can explore what percent of George Washington's army was sick at any given time as they describe life as a solider living through all kinds of conditions; students studying World War II can compare wartime food rations to food consumption in the U.S. today.

Students can also be quite creative in writing math sidebars for popular fiction of their choice.

Name _____ Date _____

What's Been Untold?

Directions: Use the questions to plan mathematical sidebars for a story.

Name of the original story: _____

Record ideas for how math is part of the story that has not been told.

_____

_____

_____

What ideas about the setting can you include in a math sidebar?

_____

_____

_____

What ideas about the time and place of the story can you include in a math sidebar?

_____

_____

_____

What ideas about the problems the characters face can you include in a math sidebar?

_____

_____

_____

How do the math sidebars help you better understand the story?

_____

_____

_____

Points of Entry

Model Lesson: Story Enders

Model Lesson Overview

This strategy can be used at any point in a story; students will be entering the story at the end and working backward. Working backward is often used to solve mathematical problems. In this strategy, students are given the last line of a story and have to figure out what happened in the middle and beginning. Like story starters, story enders can help students begin to create, tell, and then enjoy the different stories their peers create from common story enders.

Learning Objectives

K–2

- Uses discussions with teachers and other students to understand problems

- Assumes roles that exhibit concentration and contribute to the action of dramatizations based on personal experience and heritage, imagination, literature, and history

3–5

- Understands the basic language of logic in mathematical situations

- Assumes roles that exhibit concentration and contribute to the action of dramatizations based on personal experience and heritage, imagination, literature, and history

6–8

- Formulates a problem, determines information required to solve the problem, chooses methods for obtaining this information, and sets limits for acceptable solutions

- Interacts as an invented character in improvised and scripted scenes

Materials

- *Story Enders Planner* (page 221, storyenders.pdf)

Points of Entry (cont.)

Preparation

Identify scenarios that will elicit students' thinking about working backward. For instance, ask students questions such as, "If someone new to the school were given written directions from the school's front door to our classroom door, how could those directions be used to figure out how to get back to the front door?" or, "If you had to be at a special event at 7:00 in the morning, how would you decide when to wake up?"

Identify a piece of writing with which students are familiar. It could be a classic tale or contemporary fiction. Mark a particularly dramatic moment in the text, such as when the clock strikes 12 o'clock in a version of *Cinderella* or when Harry Potter first enters the chamber in *Harry Potter and the Chamber of Secrets* by J. K. Rowling.

Procedure

1. Ask students if they ever work backward to solve a problem. Pose some scenarios in which students can work backward to stimulate further discussion.

2. Choose one of the story enders (see the Specific Grade Level Ideas). Tell students you are going to show them the last line of a story. Read the story ender as you display it on the board and ask students to brainstorm what may have happened before the story ended. Have students first brainstorm individually before sharing with partners. Then, have students discuss their ideas with one another.

3. Have students share their ideas with the larger group and ask such questions as, "What do you think happened before that? What title would you give this story?"

4. Explain to students that they will have the opportunity to further develop the story for this ending, but first you want to talk with them about how to tell their stories in interesting ways. Read the piece of writing you have chosen, but do so in a monotone voice. Ask students what you could do to make the story sound more interesting. Draw out ideas about the use of character voice, movement choices, and use of pauses to heighten interest. Explore the potential for engaging the audience in participating in the reading through choral moments, gestures, or the introduction of contextual sounds. Then, reread the text, adopting their suggestions. Tell students that they should tell their stories dramatically as well.

5. Have students work alone, in pairs, or in small groups to complete their stories and practice telling them. Distribute the *Story Enders Planner* (page 221) to help students plan their stories. Use the Planning Questions to guide students' thinking.

Points of Entry (cont.)

6. Invite students to include opportunities for audience interaction in their stories. This may include choral moments, character movements, and shared mathematical calculations.

7. Have students tell their stories to the class. Encourage the audience to pay close attention and identify compelling moments in the story and in the storytelling.

8. Encourage students to note the similarities and differences among the stories with the same endings. Be sure that students compare both the story plots and the mathematics.

Planning Questions

• What kind of story does this ending suggest? What mathematical ideas does it imply? Do you want to tell a story that is serious, fanciful, or adventurous?

• Who do you visualize telling this story? What character traits will you give this character? What other roles might you include?

• What mathematical problem or conflict might the character encounter? How will it be resolved? What specific events will take place to keep the story moving?

Specific Grade Level Ideas

K–2

Have students record their stories or draw pictures to help them remember what to tell next. Some possible endings include:

• *I will never forget the day I found all those pennies.*

• *At last, I counted the right number of cookies.*

• *Finally, I had enough ribbon for everyone.*

• *And when I woke up, all the circles were back where they belonged.*

Points of Entry *(cont.)*

3–5

Though many students can work independently, allow them the opportunity to first brainstorm ideas with others. Some possible endings include:

- *Finally, I woke up from the nightmare and realized that zero still existed.*
- *If I had known this was going to happen, I would have paid more attention to learning about fractions.*
- *And then I found my watch and realized I hadn't missed the party after all.*
- *I can't believe I earned so much money in one day.*

6–8

Challenge students to write their own endings to a mathematical story. Their endings can be placed in a hat and drawn by the other students. Other possible endings include:

- *And that's how I saved a billion dollars.*
- *Finally, I got the hit that would win the game and give me the highest batting average on the team.*
- *If I had known this was going to happen, I would have looked closer at the unit prices.*
- *I was dripping wet but safe, and I had learned why sewer covers were round.*

Name _____   Date _____

Story Enders Planner

Directions: Use the organizer to help you plan your story based on a story ender.

Who?

List characters and specific character traits for each character.

Where?

List details about the setting.

Ending

Beginning

Write about what happens in the beginning of the story and how it relates to mathematics.

Middle

Write about what happens in the middle of the story and how it relates to mathematics.

Visual Arts

Visual Arts

Understanding Visual Arts

The importance of images and visual media in contemporary culture is changing what it means to be literate in the 21st century. Today's society is highly visual, and visual imagery is no longer supplemental to other forms of information. New digital technologies have made it possible for almost anyone to create and share visual media. Yet the pervasiveness of images and visual media does not necessarily mean that individuals are able to critically view, use, and produce visual content. Individuals must develop these essential skills in order to engage capably in a visually-oriented society. Visual literacy empowers individuals to participate fully in a visual culture.

—Association of College & Research Libraries (2011)

We are bombarded with images on a daily basis, and although we have become more skilled at reading the nontextual representation of ideas, our visual-literacy abilities need to develop further. Why, then, is education so often text based? Working with images can provide opportunities for students to observe, notice details, and make meaning. Visual work can communicate nuances that words cannot. In this section, we see how students can use visual art as a language that is more unstructured than text.

Particular to visual arts is hands-on work with various materials. Visual artists use their art in many ways to create narratives, observe, explore patterns, translate, represent, and juxtapose ideas using visual communication. Using the elements of art— *line, form, shape, color, texture,* and *pattern*—students can investigate and create visual representations of ideas. They can also create images as a way to tell what they know.

Integrating the visual arts is a way to help students see and express mathematical principles visually. Incorporating visual imagery into your math lessons can help make mathematical concepts more tangible, accessible, and engaging (Dacey and Lynch 2007).

Also, when students process visual information as well as verbal, they are using different parts of the brain. Allan Paivio suggests that learning can be expanded by the inclusion of visual imagery, allowing for what he termed "dual coding" (quoted in Reed 2010).

Marianne Freiberger (2005) notes that "maths and art are just two different languages that can be used to express the same ideas." Moving between visual and numerical concepts can develop representational fluency and enhance students' ability to work with symbol systems. The visual arts are a natural fit with mathematics as images allow students to work in new ways with ideas of scale, perspective, patterns, and more. As students translate mathematical ideas into visual form, they draw on higher-order thinking skills such as synthesis and evaluation (Dacey and Eston 2002). All curricular areas have visual aspects, so providing students with the opportunity to work with multiple representations of content is easy to incorporate and will allow students new ways to engage with and access mathematical ideas.

Visual Arts (cont.)

Strategies for Visual Arts

∞ Visual Narrative

In this strategy, students create and arrange images in sequence to tell a story or create a narrative. The story can be told through images alone, or the pictures can interact with text. Students' understanding of curricular content is enhanced as they create visual narratives that demonstrate and/or apply their learning. Often, creating a visual narrative makes it easier for students to grasp connections and clarify their thinking, which they can then translate into text. Students can illustrate mathematical concepts, translating their understanding into visual form.

Visual narratives can culminate in the creation of simple books, digital image essays, magazines, storyboards, comics, and other formats that are easy to make. This allows students to compose content, applying and articulating their knowledge in new ways. Teaching artist and researcher Wendy Strauch-Nelson (2011, 9) notes that students "seemed drawn to the complementary relationship between the linear style of words and the layered nature of images."

∞ Visual Patterns

Lynn Steen, in the classic book *On the Shoulders of Giants: New Approaches to Numeracy*, describes mathematics as the language and science of patterns (1990). Artists often work with patterns. Pattern is considered one of the fundamental communication elements in the visual-arts principles of design. These design elements include line, shape, form, texture, pattern, and color. Through the visual arts, students can demonstrate a variety of curricular concepts by creating and manipulating patterns. Working with patterns can guide observations, and shifting patterns can generate interest and curiosity. Students can track and document patterns in the world through artistic representations that capture cycles of change. In mathematics, students can use visual patterns to deepen and extend their understanding of numbers and operations.

∞ Representation

Students investigate the ability of the visual arts to communicate information and ideas in compelling ways, to direct our attention, and to add layers of meaning. When students represent concepts through visual art, they translate their understanding into new forms, taking ownership of ideas and engaging with symbolism and metaphor.

David McCandless (2010) notes in his TED talk that we are overwhelmed by information and what he calls "data glut." He suggests that we work with representing data in new ways that prompt us to use our eyes. In this strategy, students create visual work, such as visual essays or infographics, to depict information.

One example of the power of representation comes from Adam Hollander, the executive creative producer for Brand Marketers in New York. He created an installation on the National Mall of the Washington Monument of 857 desks representing the number of students who drop out of school every hour. Adeshina Emmanuel (2012) commented, "Everybody hears that 857 number, but it doesn't really mean anything until you're able to see it." The image of hundreds of empty desks prompted visitors to sign a petition demanding that politicians address this trend.

∞ Observation

Visual images can provide opportunities for students to observe, attend to details, and make meaning. As cited by Hilary Landorf (2006), Housen and Yenawine found that close observation and discussion of works of art "measurably increases observation skills, evidential reasoning, and speculative abilities, and the ability to find multiple solutions to complex problems" (29). Students can focus and expand their observations, both through the study of the works of others and in the creation of their own visual work. Through deep observation of the work of a variety of well-known artists, students can investigate how artists use mathematical concepts in the preparation, creation, and representation of visual ideas. Through this strategy, students can recognize the natural fit between mathematics and the visual arts.

∞ Mixed Media

This strategy allows students to experiment with putting a range of materials together in new ways. Students manipulate materials, experiment with the juxtaposition of materials, and create two- or three-dimensional pieces such as mobiles, collages, assemblages, dioramas, and digital installations. Students test and explore ideas in experiential, hands-on ways; make choices about how they will use materials to communicate; and explore cause-and-effect relationships in the process of working with different media. The use of multiple representations is essential to the development of flexible mathematical strategies.

Visual Narrative

Model Lesson: Storyboards

Model Lesson Overview

In this strategy, students use visual narrative as a problem-solving tool. Students decide how to break up a problem into meaningful scenes. Then, they combine text with artwork to solve and explain the problem. Students may break up their problems into three scenes with three pieces of artwork, or they could have many scenes and choose to present their narratives through digital storytelling.

Standards

K–2

- Draws pictures to represent problems

- Explains to others how she or he went about solving a numerical problem

- Selects prospective ideas for works of art

3–5

- Uses a variety of strategies to understand problem situations

- Represents problem situations in a variety of forms

- Selects prospective ideas for works of art

6–8

- Understands how to break a complex problem into simpler parts or use a similar problem type to solve a problem

- Represents problem situations in and translates among oral, written, concrete, pictorial, and graphical forms

- Knows how visual, spatial, and temporal concepts integrate with content to communicate intended meaning in one's artworks

9–12

- Uses a variety of strategies to understand new mathematical content and to develop more efficient solution methods or problem extensions

- Understands connections between equivalent representations and corresponding procedures of the same problem situation or mathematical concept

- Applies various subjects, symbols, and ideas in one's artworks

Visual Narrative *(cont.)*

Materials

- Visual narrative sample (comic, graphic novel, storyboard)
- Chart paper
- Scissors
- Glue
- *Storyboard Planner* (page 232, storyboard.pdf)
- Butcher paper
- Sticky notes *(optional)*
- Art supplies (markers, crayons, paint, clay, etc.)
- Access to a computer with software that can combine text and visuals *(optional)*

Preparation

Choose mathematical problems you would like students to solve and write them on chart paper. Be sure the problems are at the right level of challenge so that students will wrestle with mathematical ideas but not so challenging that they become frustrated. Identify one problem to solve as a class to model the strategy. Identify an example of visual narrative to share with students, such as a comic, graphic novel, or storyboard. Other ideas are provided in the Specific Grade Level Ideas.

Procedure

1. Explain that a visual narrative is a story told in a sequence of images and text. Show the visual narrative example that you chose and discuss how the artist may have decided to break the story or information into panels and how to sequence the panels.

2. Tell students that they will be creating a storyboard to help them solve a mathematical problem and explain their thinking. Present the problem you have identified.

3. As a class, decide how to break the problem into sections. Ask students questions such as "What do we know? What do we need to find?" Mark on the chart paper to show where the problem will be divided.

4. Cut the problem apart and glue each section in order on a long piece of butcher paper and display the sectioned problem for the class.

5. Talk together as a class about how illustrations would help make each section meaningful. Make a sketch of what the artwork might look like above the text on the butcher paper.

Visual Narrative (cont.)

6. Have students solve a new problem individually or in pairs using the visual narrative strategy. Distribute the *Storyboard Planner* (page 232) for students to record their thinking. Students can add sticky notes to record ideas about which artistic medium they want to use and later replace the notes with illustrations. Use the Planning Questions to guide students' thinking.

7. Have students review their storyboards to evaluate how well they conveyed the strategy for solving their problem. Have students edit or add visual detail as necessary.

8. Have students finalize their work by creating a story page for each scene they planned using markers, crayons, paint, etc., and staple the pages together to make a book. Or have students do this using software that allows for the combination of text and illustrations.

9. Provide time for students to share their work with one another.

10. Consider having students share their visual narratives with fellow students, omitting the problem-solving information to challenge them to decipher the problems depicted in the images.

11. Have students discuss the process of making their visual narratives, using the Questions for Discussion.

Planning Questions

- How will you break the problem into meaningful parts?

- What images might you create to help you solve the problem?

- What images or text might you use to explain your solution process?

- What medium will you choose to create your artwork, and why (colored pencils, paint, photographs, or drawing programs on a computer)?

Questions for Discussion

- How did you choose your visual images?

- How did the images you used influence the text you included?

- How do your images and text work together?

- What did you learn about problem solving from creating your storyboard?

- As you were reading and viewing the work of others, what did you realize about problem solving?

Visual Narrative *(cont.)*

Specific Grade Level Ideas

K–2

Students can focus on the vocabulary associated with different uses of addition and subtraction. For example, students can illustrate the different actions of separating from or adding to, allowing images to add visual details to the story. Students can also use this strategy to explore time. They can add numbers and hands to clocks and create visuals that illustrate and annotate what they do at different times of the day.

3–5

Students can turn their storyboards into digital stories. As well as problem solving, students can create a visual and compelling narrative, explaining particular computational strategies and why they work.

6–8

Students can use visual narratives to reflect on mathematical concepts such as variability or to tell stories of how mathematics is used in the workplace. Students can do research online, video or photograph examples, and interview people in the field, adding images and text that capture the essence of mathematical concepts. If time allows, they can then create digital storybooks or use presentation software to present their narratives.

9–12

In addition to the 6–8 Specific Grade Level Ideas, students can create storyboards to explore mathematical ideas such as the Fibonacci sequence or functions. They can also create tutorials that are not lectures but truly visual essays for other students. They can create a classroom video library of such resources.

Name _____ Date _____

Storyboard Planner

Directions: Plan your scenes on this storyboard.

Illustration			
Text			

Visual Patterns

Model Lesson: Curve Stitching

Model Lesson Overview

Curve stitching, or string art, was popularized in the 1960s. It involves sewing colored thread through holes or wrapping thread around nails or pins. The positioning of the holes, nails, or pins leads to the creation of geometric patterns and the recognition of algebraic relationships. Straight lines are combined in ways that can create the image of a curve. A wide range of students will be able to participate in this craft. Discussion is crucial to helping students discover the mathematical concepts in this strategy.

Standards

K–2

- Extends simple patterns
- Uses visual structures and functions of art to communicate ideas

3–5

- Recognizes a wide variety of patterns and the rules that explain them
- Uses visual structures and functions of art to communicate ideas

6–8

- Understands various representations of patterns and functions and the relationships among them
- Knows some of the effects of various visual structures and functions of art

9–12

- Understands the concept of a function as the correspondences between the elements of two sets
- Knows specific techniques and skills used in different art forms

Materials

- *Circle with 10 Points* (page 240, 10points.pdf)
- Rulers
- *Circle with 12 Points* (page 241, 12points.pdf)

- *Circle with 23 Points* (page 242, 23points.pdf)
- Colored pencils, colored chalk, ribbons or streamers, thread or yarn, cardboard or wood, paint, nails, hammer *(optional)*

Visual Patterns *(cont.)*

Preparation

Decide on the materials that you want students to use; colored pencils on paper, colored chalk on blacktop, ribbons or streamers held by students, thread or yarn on cardboard, paint on paper as well as nails and embroidery thread on wood are all potential options. Make choices that best fit your students and supplies. Note that paper and pencil are readily available, though nails and yarn allow students to explore a variety of options on the same frame by unwinding the yarn and starting again. If curve stitching is new to you, take time to explore some ideas yourself.

For differentiation, you can assign number rules (i.e., +5 or +6) or have students make the choice. These activities can be completed in pairs or individually. Other ideas are provided in the Specific Grade Level Ideas.

Procedure

1. Draw the *Circle with 10 Points* (page 240) on the board to demonstrate for students how to connect the dots using a +3 number rule. Start at 0 and, using a ruler or other straight edge, draw a line from 0 to 3. Then, do the same from 3 to 6, 6 to 9, 9 to 2, and so on until all the unique connecting lines have been drawn.

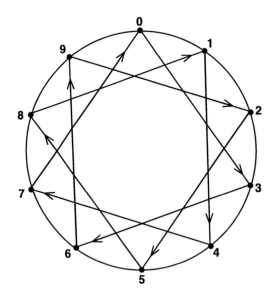

2. Ask students to share anything they noticed or discovered about the pattern. Record responses for students to refer to throughout the lesson.

3. Tell students that they will be exploring other number rules by creating their own patterns. Assign or have students choose a number rule. Have students brainstorm a list of "I wonder..." statements about the new rule and record these ideas for students to reference throughout the lesson. For example, say, "I wonder if it will use all the points," or "I wonder if it will make a pattern."

Visual Patterns (cont.)

4. Distribute several copies of *Circle with 10 Points* to students. Use the Planning Questions to discuss. Provide students time to explore their number rules, using pencils and rulers to skip-count and draw lines to connect the dots on their circle.

5. Have students gather to discuss their findings and link back to their initial "I wonder..." statements whenever possible.

6. Display *Circle with 12 Points* (page 241). Have students suggest number rules and explain any predictions they can make about the designs that will result. Encourage students to discuss and justify their predictions.

7. Distribute several copies of the *Circle with 12 Points* to students and have them explore their ideas. This time, suggest the use of colored pencils and the notion of repeating rules on the same circle. For example, a +3 number rule could be placed on the same circle with a +4 number rule, or a +4 number rule that begins at 1 could be placed on the same circle as a +4 rule that begins at 0, using a different color for each rule. Encourage students to explore a variety of colors and combinations. *Circle with 23 Points* (page 242) is available for students who wish to explore a greater number of points.

8. Have students choose the combination that they find most artistically pleasing and write an explanation of why they chose it and the mathematics illustrated within it.

9. If possible, have students create a more permanent artifact. Have students place the *Circle with 23 Points* on a piece of wood and use a pencil to make a hole through the paper at each point to mark on the wood below. Hammer a nail into the wood at each mark and wind colored yarn or embroidery thread around the nails to create lines. Then, have students paint their artifacts so the pattern remains intact once the paint dries.

10. Use the Questions for Discussion to help students articulate the mathematical concepts in this activity.

Planning Questions

- What number rule do you want to use? Why?

- What prediction might you make about the design that will result?

- Based on the design you just formed, what number rule do you want to try next? Why?

Visual Patterns *(cont.)*

Questions for Discussion

- What do you notice about the numbers you land on for the +3 rule on the *Circle with 10 Points*?

- What connections can you make between these numbers and the multiplication table for three?

- What do you think a +5 design would look like on a circle with 15 points?

- What must be true for a polygon to emerge from a + rule?

- How many different designs do you think there could be on a circle with 8 points? What would you predict about a circle with 29 points?

- Does it matter if the number of points is prime or composite?

- How could you use math to design specific aesthetic features in your next creation?

Visual Patterns *(cont.)*

Specific Grade Level Ideas

K–2

Students can focus on counting, skip counting, and addition and subtraction. Introduce students to curve stitching by giving 10 students a number sign (0–9) to wear. Then, have students arrange themselves in order in a circle. Give an 11th student a roll of string, ribbon, or crepe paper, and identify that student as the designer. Direct the designer to give the end of the ribbon to the student wearing the zero sign and then to follow a +2 number rule (i.e., the designer counts two students and has the second student hold on to the ribbon). The designer continues around the circle until he or she is back at the starting point. Have the other students count "2, 4, 6, 8, 10" as the stitching is formed. Ask students if they notice anything about the numbers they are saying aloud and the numbers the students are wearing. Point out to students that only the ones digit is given, so for 10, they only see the zero. Then, explore +1 and +5 rules.

First- and second-grade students can explore number rules using the *Circle with 10 Points* on paper, as described in the activity. Encourage extensive discussion as students discover patterns. For example, the +8 pattern is the same as the +2 pattern because each time, the 10 points are being separated into a group of eight and a group of two. Or as one second-grade student observed, "When you go back 8, it is the same as going forward 2. So, they are the same but backward."

Provide hands-on practice by giving students cardboard that has 10 holes punched in a circle. Have students lace yarn or embroidery thread through the holes to create curved stitching patterns.

Visual Patterns *(cont.)*

3–5

Students can connect the designs that are the same in the circles to the inverse relationship between addition and subtraction. They can also use their understanding of multiples and factors to make predictions about designs if they know the number rule, the number of points, and that the rule starts at 0. For example, they know that $4 \times 5 = 20$, so they should be able to predict that a +4 rule will result in a regular pentagon on a circle with 20 points. Differences between prime and composite numbers can also be discussed.

Students can explore designs that result from using right angles and focus on measurement and the relationships among lines and curves. Have students trace an index-card corner to make a right angle and measure the same number of equidistant points on each line segment. Students then draw lines from one segment to the other. Have students begin by connecting the top point on the vertical segment with the first point on the horizontal segment. An example is shown below. Students can then investigate the design possibilities when they combine these configurations or when they change the measures of the lengths and angles.

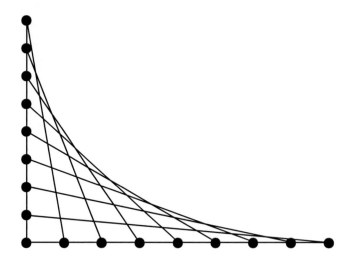

Visual Patterns *(cont.)*

6–8

In addition to the 3–5 Specific Grade Level Ideas, students can explore linear algebraic relationships. For example, if students start at 5 on the *Circle with 10 Points* and follow a +6 number rule and do not stop when drawing over the same line, at what number would they be after drawing 15 lines? Help students identify the $y = 6x + 5$ equation to describe the relationship between the number of times the +6 number rule is applied, starting at 5, and the number at which they end. After generating several such rules, have students explain the meaning of the slope and the *y*-intercept in this real-world application.

Students can also use their knowledge of circumference and their ability to measure internal angles around the center to mark their own equidistant points on the circle.

9–12

Some students may want to do research online about modular arithmetic developed by Leonhard Euler and later advanced by Carl Friedrich Gauss and connect the notion of equivalent classes to these circles. Encourage students to consider a variety of designs and not limit themselves to circles or right angles.

Name _____ Date _____

Circle with 10 Points

Directions: Make a pattern using a number rule of your choice. Then, on a separate sheet of paper, explain why you chose this rule and the mathematics illustrated by your rule.

0
●

9
●

●**1**

8 ●

●**2**

7 ●

●**3**

●
6

●**4**

●
5

Name _____ Date _____

Circle with 12 Points

Directions: Make a pattern using number rules of your choice. Then, on a separate sheet of paper, explain why you chose those rules and the mathematics illustrated by each rule.

0

11 **1**

10 **2**

9 **3**

8 **4**

7 **5**

6

Name _____ Date _____

Circle with 23 Points

Directions: Make a pattern using number rules of your choice. Then, on a separate sheet of paper, explain why you chose those rules and the mathematics illustrated by each rule.

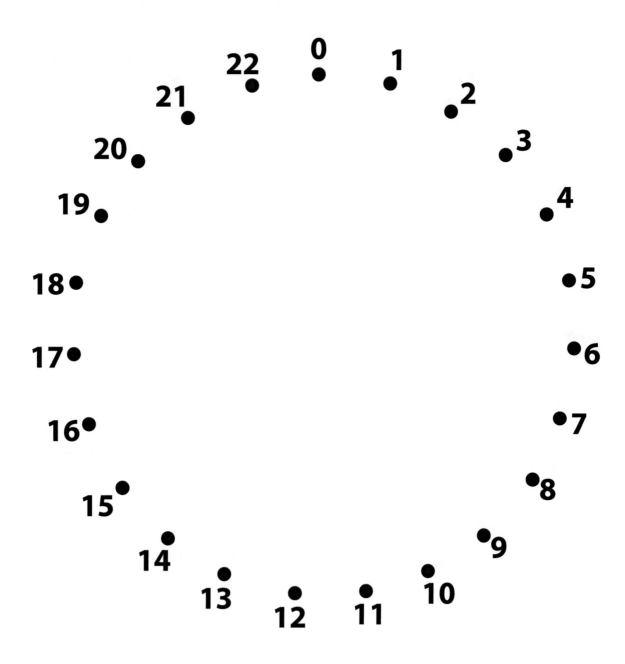

Representation

Model Lesson: Visualize the Data

Model Lesson Overview

Translating data into visual form through the visual arts can help to tell the story of data in fresh ways. In this strategy, students collect data and use visual art to highlight ideas within the numbers, incorporating visual means to provide context, comparison, and even commentary. Students collect data and then create their own representations of that data, thinking about multiple ways that quantitative data can be represented. This process allows students to act as mathematicians and artists as they create their own visual-information maps.

Standards

K–2

- Collects and represents information about objects or events in simple graphs

- Knows various purposes for creating works of visual art

3–5

- Organizes and displays data in simple bar graphs, pie charts, and line graphs

- Knows various purposes for creating works of visual art

6–8

- Understands that the same set of data can be represented using a variety of tables, graphs, and symbols and that different modes of representation often convey different messages

- Distinguishes among multiple purposes for creating works of visual art

9–12

- Selects and uses the best method of representing and describing a set of data

- Identifies intentions of those creating artworks

Materials

- Art supplies (paper, colored pencils, markers, paint, scissors, crayons, paper, magazines, etc.)

- *Data-Collection Planner* (page 248, dataplanner.pdf)

- *Visual-Representation Planner* (pages 249–250, visualplanner.pdf)

Representation *(cont.)*

Preparation

Collect a wide range of artistic materials for students to use. Decide whether to have students work individually or in groups. For older students, share with them *The Visual Display of Quantitative Information* by Edward Tufte. Tufte is known for his creative visual representation of numerical data. Refer to the Specific Grade Level Ideas for additional ideas.

Procedure

1. Tell students that one thing that mathematicians do is collect and share information. Explain to students that research is a process in which someone asks a question that they are curious about and then he or she collects information (data) to answer that question. Notify students that they are going to be mathematicians who collect data about their classmates.

2. Provide time for students to talk with a partner about questions they might ask about their classmates. Questions can be simple with only *yes* or *no* answers, such as "Do you like carrots?" or they can offer multiple answer choices, such as "What is your favorite food?"

3. Have students share their questions with the class. Record students' questions for them to reference throughout the lesson. Choose a question, and ask students to think about the data that might be gathered. This discussion helps students to further refine their questions, an important aspect of the research process. For example, when discussing the question "At what time do you go to bed?," a student might note, "It matters if it's a school night or not. I get to stay up late on Fridays." Students should then revise the question: "At what time do you go to bed on a school night?"

4. Ask students to think about how they will collect their data. Will they ask people directly and tally their findings on paper? Will they collect data via email and enter it in a spreadsheet? Will they create an online survey?

5. Have students work in pairs to complete the *Data-Collection Planner* (page 248). Once they have checked their plans with you, have them collect the data.

6. Tell students that they will create visual representations of the data they collected. Ask students how they might show results of their research, and record responses for them to refer to throughout the lesson. In addition to traditional approaches such as bar graphs, encourage students to also think about more artistic choices. For example, if four children go to bed at 8:30, the representation of data could be a picture of four children in a bed over which a clock shows the time. Encourage students to think about what they want people to see in their data and how they can represent that visually. Ask, "How might you use visual symbols to represent your data in interesting ways?"

Representation (cont.)

7. Have students complete the *Visual-Representation Planner* (pages 249–250) in pairs or individually. Once you approve their plans, offer students a choice of art materials with which to create visual representations of their findings. Encourage students to think critically about which materials they will use to create their representation.

8. Have students share their renderings and use the Questions for Discussion to discuss their findings. Encourage them to compare the different methods of representation.

Questions for Discussion

- What did you learn from the data you collected?

- What did you learn from looking at the visual representation of data?

- How did working with visual-arts materials help you think of ideas for your visual representation?

- How does the creation of an artistic work move beyond simple reporting of numerical data?

- What data might you collect next that might lead to interesting visual representations?

Specific Grade Level Ideas

K–2

Have students focus on questions that offer only two-answer choices, such as *yes or no* or *walk or run*. These simple questions will make it easier for students to keep track of the data they collect. Work with students to brainstorm images that might support the representation of their data. They can use pictures and drawings as well as make picture graphs to show their data. Encourage students to record their questions (or work with a recorder to do so) as well as a summary statement about their findings using mathematical language such as "more than," "less than," or "as much as." Have students include the number of respondents for each answer choice and a simple statement such as, "More students liked cake than cookies."

The visual representation of ideas is essential in all areas of mathematics. Students who develop strong visual images of numbers, for example, are able to see that six is one more than five or that four is less than ten. Students can also use visual representations to show information in a story problem or what they did to solve a problem.

Representation *(cont.)*

3–5

Students can pose more complex questions with a greater variety of possible answers and provide the answer choices such as, "Which vegetable do you like best: carrots, broccoli, tomatoes, or green beans?" Some students may be ready to pose open-ended questions such as "How do you feel about homework?" Such questions will require students to categorize the responses in a way that makes sense rather than reporting each individual response.

Encourage students to make predictions about the outcomes of their polls. Ask questions such as, "What do you think will be a typical answer to your question? What would be an unusual answer to your question?" Visual representations can be more complex as students compare and contrast and work with more nuanced ways to tell the story the data reveals. For example, have students create a cartoon that includes the findings along with more traditional representations such as bar graphs, line plots, or pie graphs. Students can work backward from the image to identify what data or questions can go with that representation.

Visual models permeate mathematics. Students can use visual representations to show relationships among numbers. They can draw bars to organize information in a word problem or number lines to organize their thinking about addition or subtraction. Expand the visual language students can use to express their understanding.

Representation *(cont.)*

6–8

Students can work with statistical data from any area of interest. They can collect data outside the classroom or compare their data to online data and discuss the impact of increasing sample size. Students could survey different classrooms or different grade levels and consider variation between the sets of data. Encourage students to depict data in traditional ways (graphs and plots) and nontraditional ways and to comment on how the different visual representations impact the communication of the mathematical ideas.

Representation of relationships is key to algebraic thinking as students are expected to make links among tables, graphs, and equations. Representation also helps students model operations with integers, discover proportional relationships, experiment with functions, and have facility with other mathematical processes.

9–12

Have students collect data that they represent in histograms and box plots related to real-world events (e.g., the number of people at a coffee shop over different times of the day), and create a nontraditional representation of the data as well. Display the representations randomly, and have students try to match the traditional mathematical representations to their nontraditional representations.

Name _____   Date _____

Data-Collection Planner

Directions: Answer the questions to help you plan for your data collection.

1. What is your research question?

   _____

   _____

2. What are the possible answer choices?

   _____

   _____

   _____

   _____

3. How will you collect and keep track of your data?

   _____

   _____

   _____

   _____

4. What predictions can you make about the answers you will collect?

   _____

   _____

   _____

   _____

Name _____ Date _____

Visual-Representation Planner

Directions: Fill in the sections using the data you collected in your research.

1. Summary of my data:

   _____

   _____

   _____

   _____

   _____

   _____

2. My ideas for a visual representation:

   _____

   _____

   _____

   _____

   _____

   _____

3. Materials I will use:

   _____

   _____

   _____

   _____

   _____

Name _____ Date _____

Visual-Representation Planner *(cont.)*

4. Sketch or description of what I want to do:

Observation

Model Lesson: Masterpiece Math

Model Lesson Overview

When focusing on the work of well-known artists or art movements, students gain an appreciation for art and its history. They can draw mathematical concepts from visual representation. This activity focuses on the work of Solomon LeWitt, who worked with a variety of media and whose work is connected to conceptual art and minimalism. For his wall art, he created guidelines or simple diagrams of what others were to draw or paint directly on walls. Students follow and create directions for similar works using ideas involving geometry and measurement. Ways to connect the work of other visual artists to mathematics are provided in the Specific Grade Level Ideas. All works referenced can be found on the Internet.

Standards

K–2
- Understands the basic properties of simple geometric shapes and similarities and differences between simple geometric shapes
- Identifies specific works of art as belonging to particular cultures, times, and places

3–5
- Understands basic geometric language for describing and naming shapes
- Understands basic properties of figures
- Identifies specific works of art as belonging to particular cultures, times, and places

6–8
- Understands the defining properties of triangles
- Understands the historical and cultural contexts of a variety of art objects

Materials

- LeWitt art
- *Sol LeWitt Plan* (page 256, lewittplan.pdf)
- Mural paper *(optional)*
- Paint, colored pencils, or crayons *(optional)*
- File folders *(optional)*
- Rulers

Observation (cont.)

Preparation

Become familiar with the work of Solomon LeWitt, known as Sol, by conducting an Internet search or visiting the website of the Massachusetts Museum of Contemporary Art (http://www.massmoca.org/lewitt/). Select a few wall murals to share with students and one on which to focus their attention. At the end of the activity, students will create their own LeWitt-style drawings with instructions. The scope of the work is up to you. Depending on what you decide, provide mural paper and tempera paints, colored pencils or crayons, and regular plain paper, or have students complete their final drawings outside of class.

Read the Specific Grade Level Ideas for other ways to connect to the work of visual artists. These activities could be explored over time or combined at a learning station.

Procedure

1. Write the following LeWitt-type directions on the board. Read the directions to students and have them make a sketch based on them. Encourage students to work independently, perhaps creating a private office space by placing file folders upright around their papers. (Adapt the directions to better meet the readiness of your students.)

   Draw two rectangles and one triangle.

   The lengths of the sides of the triangle should all be different.

   There should be four thick lines, each one-inch long, drawn in one of the rectangles.

2. Have students share their sketches and identify how they are different and how they are similar.

3. Tell students that an artist named Solomon LeWitt, known as Sol, wrote directions for wall drawings that others then followed to create murals. Share some images of LeWitt's work with students, asking them to note common colors and shapes. Draw their attention to the expansiveness of these wall drawings. Point out when and where these murals were created.

4. Show a single image of a LeWitt mural. Ask students to talk with a partner about the directions LeWitt may have written so that others could create this work. Have partners take notes about their ideas and provide time for several pairs to present their thinking. Discuss the variety of directions. Ask, "Which directions would be best if the goal was to create an exact copy?" Tell students that LeWitt was open to the interpretation of his directions. Ask, "Which directions would be best if this was his intention?"

Observation (cont.)

5. Tell students that they will now create their own LeWitt drawings by first writing the directions and then drawing an image based on the directions. Distribute and have students complete *Sol LeWitt Plan* (page 256). As students work, use the Planning Questions to guide their thinking.

6. Once you approve their plans, provide the materials and time for students to either create the drawings in class or as homework. Create a display of the completed projects, along with their directions.

Planning Questions

- What shapes, colors, and lines do you want to use? Why?

- How will you use measurements and geometric terms to describe your picture?

- Do you want your directions to be exact or open to interpretation?

- Are there other ways to describe this?

- How might you use a code or diagram to represent this information?

Specific Grade Level Ideas

K–2

Students can explore the style of Sol LeWitt by using directions with references to color, number, length, position, and basic two-dimensional shapes. They can also include references to terms that describe spatial relations such as *above*, *below*, and *between*. Measurement directions should be in whole units, and the units may be informal or standard.

Other masterpieces to observe to stimulate mathematical ideas include the still life paintings of Robert Seldon Duncanson such as *Still Life with Fruits and Nuts*. Ask questions such as, "How could you tell whether someone handed you a large nut or a small apple if your eyes were closed? Why do you think the artist organized the shapes in this way?" Then, ask questions or have students pose questions about the number of apples, grapes, currants, and nuts, such as, "Is each countable? How does the number of each food item compare?" Allow time for students to sketch their own still-life pictures and talk about their sketches in artistic and mathematical terms.

Have students consider *The Goldfish* by Henri Matisse, and after noting the impressionist's paint strokes and use of color, count the number of fish. Then, ask students to determine the number of eyes these fish have, even though all of them cannot be seen in the painting. If time allows, have students explore making impressionistic drawings.

Observation *(cont.)*

3–5

Students can focus on directions with references to color, number, length, and two-dimensional shapes. Directions involving measurements can include fractions of a unit as well as references to area and perimeter. Types of angles may also be included. Students can exchange directions and create their artwork based on someone else's description.

Other masterpieces to observe to stimulate mathematical ideas include the vivid quilts of Gee's Bend in Southern Alabama. Show pictures of the quilts and ask students how the quilts compare to others they have seen. Have students take turns describing the geometric figures in one of the quilts as listeners try to identify the quilt that is depicted. Students can create their own similar geometric designs with construction paper.

Show students one of Georges Seurat's paintings such as *Sunday Afternoon on the Island of La Grande Jatte*. Have them first look at it from far away and then more closely until they can see all of the small dots of contrasting colors. Have students determine a method for estimating the number of dots needed to make this picture and present their findings to the class. (Note that while students will not use formal proportional reasoning, they can count the dots in a small section, estimate the number of sections that size, and then multiply.) Have students use dots to create their own images.

Observation *(cont.)*

6–8

Students can focus on directions with reference to proportional relationships, special properties of triangles, and transformations. Additionally, students can explore the proportional relationships within a person's face. How widely set are the eyes? What is the variation among people's face lengths? Does it relate to the widths of faces? Have students conduct research on the Internet, in art books, or experimentally by measuring the faces of people they know and combining their data. Next, have them explore the proportional relationships within the faces in famous masterpieces. For example, students can compare the face drawn by Mary Stevenson Cassatt in *Young Woman in Green* with Pablo Picasso's cubist painting *Woman in a Blue Hat*. Students can also explore the caricature-like ways Kabuki actors are portrayed in the woodblock prints of Toshusai Sharaku. Have students consider how the proportions in these faces suggest that they are caricatures. Students who wish to explore such relationships further may research the Vitruvian man drawn by Leonardo daVinci and the notion of the golden rectangle.

Name _____ Date _____

Sol LeWitt Plan

Directions: Use this planning sheet to record the directions for your drawing, the materials you will use, and a sketch of how the drawing will look.

My directions:

_____

_____

_____

_____

_____

The materials I will use:

_____

_____

_____

_____

My sketch:

Mixed Media

Model Lesson: Code of the Khipu Assemblage

Model Lesson Overview

The ancient Inca civilization of South America did not have a written language. To keep records of their important information, the Inca and their ancestors used knots and colored cords to make a *khipu*. Khipu, which originates from the Quechua language of the Inca, means "knot." The knots represented numbers using a base-ten system. In this strategy, students learn how to represent numbers using this system and choose three important numbers in their lives to represent. Students then create an assemblage: a two- or three-dimensional piece composed of a variety of objects. Students will begin with the creation of their khipu and will incorporate a range of found items such as postcards, photographs, and artifacts that are related to what the numbers mean to the students.

Standards

K–2

- Understands symbolic, concrete, and pictorial representations of numbers
- Uses base-ten concepts to compare whole-number relationships and represent them in flexible ways
- Knows how different media, techniques, and processes are used to communicate ideas, experiences, and stories

3–5

- Understands the basic meaning of place value
- Uses models to identify, order, and compare numbers
- Knows how different media, techniques, and processes are used to communicate ideas, experiences, and stories

6–8

- Understands the characteristics and properties of the set of rational numbers and its subsets
- Understands the structure of numeration systems that are based on numbers other than 10
- Knows how the qualities and characteristics of art media, techniques, and processes can be used to enhance communication of experiences and ideas

Mixed Media *(cont.)*

Materials

- *Khipu Numbers* (page 263, khipu.pdf)

- String, yarn, or cloth strips

- *My Khipu* (pages 264–265, mykhipu.pdf)

- Art and craft supplies

- Glue, plaster, and/or tape

- Posterboard or large construction paper (one per student)

Preparation

Familiarize yourself with *khipu* by conducting an Internet search and by reading *Khipu Numbers* (page 263), which shows how the knots were used to represent numbers. Note that through differences in the placement, color, the way the knot was tied, and the attachment of the cords, it is believed that khipus provided numerical records related to such things as population, crops, and weapons. You may wish to practice tying a few of the knots yourself. Download pictures or prepare actual examples to share with students.

As students are likely to want to bring in items from home to add to their assemblages, plan for a two-day exploration for this activity. For students who are interviewing their families about their history, plan one day earlier in the week and one day later in the week. Create a letter for guardians that tells them about the project, asking them to talk about these numbers with the children and asking them to have the children bring related artifacts to school.

Procedure

1. Engage students by asking them to line up according to their exact age from youngest to oldest without using any speaking or writing. Debrief the activity by asking students to describe the strategies they used to decide where they should stand.

2. Tell students that a long time ago, there were people who used stones, gestures, pictures, and knots to communicate numbers because they didn't have a written language. Explain that the Inca were such a people and that they developed a complex system for keeping track of their numerical data. Explain what a khipu is, telling students that many Inca khipus were large and showed several numbers. Many believe that characteristics such as the color and placement of the strings identified the category of the number.

Mixed Media *(cont.)*

3. Display pictures or examples of khipus you have prepared. Distribute *Khipu Numbers* (page 263), and have students talk in pairs about how the knots represent the numbers.

4. Have students share their thinking about how the knots are used to represent numbers and the differences between the way the Inca represented numbers and the way we do today. Use the Questions for Discussion to guide students' thinking.

5. Provide students with string, yarn, or cloth strips to practice tying the knots used in making khipus.

6. Tell students that they will be creating an assemblage with their khipus. They will create two- or three-dimensional artistic compositions using one of their khipu numbers as a central component.

7. Distribute *My Khipu* (pages 264–265) and have students use it to record their thinking. Have students identify numbers that are important in their lives as described in the Specific Grade Level Ideas. Provide time for students to determine their numbers and objects they may associate with the numbers they identified. Ask students to consider what else they may want to add to their assemblages to illustrate the importance of their chosen numbers. Use the Planning Questions to guide students' thinking.

8. Provide time for students to create their assemblages using art and craft supplies, found objects, pictures (found or created), or artifacts from home. Have them tape or glue their khipu number to the construction paper or poster board and include other objects that suggest experiences that relate to the numbers. For example, a student may want to represent the number 1935, the year her great-grandmother passed through Ellis Island. She can add a picture of Ellis Island and a small umbrella (such as those found in tropical drinks) to represent the fact that her great-grandmother worked at an umbrella factory when she came to this country. A pinecone could be added to represent the woods her grandmother missed.

9. Encourage students to also include other ways to represent their numbers, such as within our own system, in expanded form or scientific notation, as word names, or with symbols they create themselves. They could also make pictures of base-ten or number-line models. Such representations could be written on bright pieces of paper to add interest to the assemblage.

Mixed Media *(cont.)*

10. Encourage students to experiment with the different choices they can make about the materials to include and where to place the different items.

11. Have students write an artist's statement describing the choices they made as they represented the numbers and their meanings in the creation of their assemblages. Provide time for students to share their important numbers.

Questions for Discussion

- What do you need to know to be able to read these numbers?

- Why did the Inca need to show several knots to tell how many ones, tens, or hundreds there were? Why do we not need to do this in our system?

- Why do you think these people chose to organize numbers in tens? Why might other societies have chosen fives (digits on one hand or foot), eights (spaces between digits on two hands or feet), or twelves (approximate number of moons in a year)?

- How did the Inca represent zero? Why do you think that throughout the world, a written symbol for zero was invented much later than other numerals, even after there were symbols for a million? (The notion of a placeholder is a complex, abstract idea.)

Planning Questions

- What numbers are most important to you?

- What objects, pictures, or photos might you add to the assemblage that relate to these numbers?

- How else could you represent these numbers in written form?

- How will the placement of your items enhance visual interest? How will you think about color as you decide where to place objects?

Mixed Media *(cont.)*

Specific Grade Level Ideas

K–2

Making the knots will be challenging for younger students. They can use different types of beads or sizes of washers and tie them onto the strings or just tie single knots for all of the values. If making knots is too difficult, have students use carved potato stamps and paint to print symbols. Then, they can glue, tape, or paste the strips of printed paper onto their assemblages. Second-grade students can explore making the knots with supervision.

Kindergarten students can explore numbers 1–20, first-grade students can represent numbers 1–100, and second-grade students can use numbers to 999. Numbers that are important to them may include their ages, the number of people in their families, their birth months and dates, their house or apartment numbers, or the number of students in their class.

Mixed media can also be used to represent any mathematical idea such as shapes in the world.

Mixed Media *(cont.)*

3–5

Students can focus on their family history. Have them interview their families about significant events in their history or heritage and the years (or approximate years) in which these events occurred. Have students choose three of these dates to use in their assemblages. Ask more advanced questions about the way numbers are represented in the khipus. For example, ask, "How would you show 1,034 using knots? How many knots would you need to represent the number 584? What is the smallest number you can represent on a khipu using 11 knots?"

As a follow-up, have students work with subcategories of data. For example, students can collect data about the number of students in each grade at their school. They can make a drawing that shows these numbers in relationship to one another. Dots on a long vertical line could represent the total number of students in the school. Curved lines stemming from this line could be drawn for each grade in the school. Dots would then be drawn on each of these lines to represent the number of students in each grade. Challenge students to decode others' khipus to determine the number and to make conjectures about what the number represents.

Mixed media can also be used to represent any mathematical idea such as relationships among measurement units.

6–8

Students can further explore how the khipus represent related data using subcategory strings. Additionally, Ascher and Ascher (1997) suggest thinking about a cash register receipt to explore the planning of a khipu. As they indicate, there are a variety of data that might be on such a receipt: date, price of each item, total cost of the items, tax, total charge, and change. It can also indicate a store number and a register number. Encourage students to determine how to organize such information in a khipu. To extend this activity, have students investigate other numerical systems, such as the early Egyptian system or Chinese system, and compare it to the khipu system used by the Inca.

Mixed media can be used to represent any mathematical idea such as the probability of different events.

Khipu Numbers

More than 600 years ago, the Inca made knots on cords to represent numbers. They used these three knots:

Long knots were used in the units position. A turn is used to show the number. This knot shows the number 3.

Single knots were used in all other positions.

A figure-eight knot was used to represent 1 when it was in the units position.

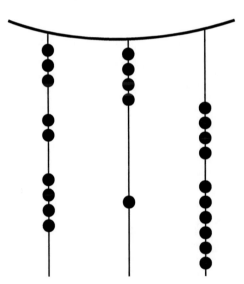

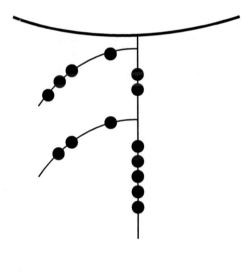

The knots were tied in clusters with spaces between them. The first cluster represented units, the next cluster represented tens, then hundreds, and so forth.

Sometimes, extra cords were tied to show subcategories. For example, this khipu could mean that there are 13 girls and 12 boys in a class of 25 students.

Name _____ Date _____

My Khipu

Directions: Make a list of numbers that are important to you. Write what each number represents. Make sketches to plan the knots on your khipu.

Number: _____

This number represents:

_____

_____

Objects I could include:

_____

_____

_____

Khipu sketch

Name _____ Date _____

My Khipu *(cont.)*

Number: _____

This number represents:

_____

_____

Objects I could include:

_____

_____

_____

Khipu sketch

References Cited

Albers, Donald J., Gerald L. Alexanderson, and Constance Reid, eds. 1990. *More Mathematical People: Contemporary Conversations*. New York: Harcourt Brace Jovanovich.

Andersen, Christopher. 2004. "Learning in 'As-If' Worlds: Cognition in Drama in Education." *Theory into Practice* 43 (4): 281–286.

Anderson, Lorin W., David R. Krathwohl, Peter W. Airasian, Kathleen A. Cruikshank, Richard E. Mayer, Paul R. Pintrich, James Raths, and Merlin C. Wittrock. 2000. *A Taxonomy for Learning, Teaching, and Assessing: A Revision of Bloom's Taxonomy of Educational Objectives*. Boston, MA: Allyn & Bacon.

Ascher, Marcia, and Robert Ascher. 1997. *Mathematics of the Incas: Code of the Quipu*. Mineola, NY: Dover Publications.

Association of College & Research Libraries. 2011. "ACRL Visual Literacy Competency Standards for Higher Education." Accessed October 10, 2012. www.ala.org/acrl /standards/visualliteracy.

Baker, Beth. 2012. "Arts Education." *CQ Researcher* 22: 253–276.

Bamberger, Jeanne. 2000. "Music, Math and Science: Towards an Integrated Curriculum." *Journal for Learning through Music* Summer 2000: 32–35.

Bellisario, Kerrie, and Lisa Donovan with Monica Prendergast. 2012. "Voices from the Field: Teachers' Views on the Relevance of Arts Integration." Unpublished manuscript. Cambridge, MA: Lesley University.

Burnaford, Gail, with Sally Brown, James Doherty, and H. James McLaughlin. 2007. *Arts Integration, Frameworks, Research and Practice*. Washington, DC: Arts Education Partnership.

Cahill, Bryon. 2006. "Ready, Set, Write!" *Writing* 29 (1): 12.

Carpenter, Siri. 2010. "Body of Thought: How Trivial Sensations Can Influence Reasoning, Social Judgment, and Perception." *Scientific American Mind* 38–45.

Catterall, James S., and Lynn Waldorf. 1999. "Chicago Arts Partnerships in Education: Summary Evaluation." Accessed January 2, 2013. http://artsedge.kennedy-center.org /champions/pdfs/CAPE.pdf.

Center for Applied Special Technology, The. Accessed October 10, 2012. http://www.cast .org/about/index.html.

Chen, Weiyun. 2001. "Description of an Expert Teacher's Constructivist-Oriented Teaching: Engaging Students' Critical Thinking in Learning Creative Dance." *Research Quarterly for Exercise and Sport* 72 (4): 366–75.

References Cited (cont.)

Collins, Anne M. 2012a. *50 Leveled Math Problems Level 5.* Huntington Beach, CA: Shell Education.

———. 2012b. *50 Leveled Math Problems Level 6.* Huntington Beach, CA: Shell Education.

Collins, Polly. 2008. "Using Poetry throughout the Curriculum." *Kappa Delta Pi Record* 44 (2): 81–84.

Dacey, Linda. 2012a. *50 Leveled Math Problems Level 1.* Huntington Beach, CA: Shell Education.

———. 2012b. *50 Leveled Math Problems Level 2.* Huntington Beach, CA: Shell Education.

———. 2012c. *50 Leveled Math Problems Level 3.* Huntington Beach, CA: Shell Education.

———. 2012d. *50 Leveled Math Problems Level 4.* Huntington Beach, CA: Shell Education.

Dacey Linda, and Rebeka Eston. 2002. *Show and Tell: Representing and Communicating Mathematical Ideas in K–2 Classrooms.* Sausalito, CA: Math Solutions.

Dacey, Linda, and Jayne Bamford Lynch. 2007. *Math for All: Differentiating Instruction, 3–5.* Sausalito, CA: Math Solutions.

Deasy, Richard J. 2002. *Critical Links: Learning in The Arts and Student Academic and Social Development.* Washington, DC: Arts Education Partnership.

Diaz, Gene, Lisa Donovan, and Louise Pascale. 2006. "Integrated Teaching through the Arts." Presentation given at the UNESCO World Conference on Arts Education in Lisbon, Portugal, March 8.

Donovan, Lisa, and Louise Pascale. 2012. *Integrating the Arts Across the Content Areas.* Huntington Beach, CA: Shell Education.

Dunn, Sonja. 1999. "Just What Is a Chant?" Accessed October 10, 2012. http://www.songsforteaching.com/sonjadunn/whatisachant.htm

Elliott-Johns, Susan E., David Booth, Jennifer Rowsell, Enrique Puig, and Jane Paterson. 2012. "Using Student Voices to Guide Instruction." *Voices from the Middle* 19 (3): 25–31.

Emmanuel, Adeshina. 2012. "Those 857 Desks? A Message for the Candidates." *New York Times*, June 20. http://www.nytimes.com/2012/06/21/education/857-desks-call-attention-to-dropout-problem.html?_r=1&smid=tw-share.

Erdoğan, Serap, and Gülen Baran. 2009. "A Study on The Effect of Mathematics Teaching Provided Through Drama on the Mathematics Ability of Six-Year-Old Children." *Eurasia Journal of Mathematics, Science & Technology Education* 5 (1): 79–85.

Freiberger, Marianne. 2005. "Art + Math = X." *Plus Magazine.* Accessed October 10, 2012. http://plus.maths.org/content/artmathx.

References Cited

Gadanidis, George, Janette M. Gadanidis, and Alyssa Y. Huang. 2005. "Using Humor to Gain Mathematical Insight." *Mathematics Teaching in the Middle School* 10 (5): 244–250.

Gardner, Howard. 2011. *Frames of Mind: The Theory of Multiple Intelligences*. 3rd ed. New York: Basic Books.

Garland, Trudi Hammel, and Charity Vaughan Kahn. 1995. *Math and Music: Harmonious Connections*. Palo Alto, CA: Dale Seymour Publications.

Geist, Kamile, and Eugene Geist. 2008. "Do Re Mi, 1-2-3: That's How Easy Math Can Be—Using Music to Support Emergent Mathematics." *Young Children* 63 (2): 20–25.

Growney, JoAnne. 2009. "What Poetry Is Found in Mathematics? What Possibilities Exist for Its Translation?" *Mathematical Intelligencer* 31 (4): 12–14.

Hamilton, Martha, and Mitch Weiss. 2005. *Children Tell Stories: Teaching and Using Storytelling in the Classroom*. Katonah, NY: Richard C. Owen Publishers.

Heagle, Amie I., and Ruth Anne Rehfeldt. 2006. "Teaching Perspective-Taking Skills to Typically Developing Children through Derived Relational Responding." *Journal of Early and Intensive Behavior Intervention* 3 (1): 1–34.

Heathcote, Dorothy, and Gavin Bolton. 1995. *Drama for Learning: Dorothy Heathcote's Mantle of the Expert Approach to Education*. Portsmouth, NH: Heinemann.

Herman, Corie. 2003. "Teaching the Cinquain: The Quintet Recipe." *Teachers & Writers* 34 (5): 19–21.

Hetland, Lois. 2009. "Nilaja Sun's 'No Child'... : Revealing Teaching and Learning through Theater." *Teaching Artist Journal* 7 (1): 34–39.

Hetland, Lois, Ellen Winner, Shirely Veenema, and Kimberly Sheridan. 2007. *Studio Thinking: The Real Benefits of Visual Arts Education*. New York: Teachers College Press.

Jensen, Eric P. 2001. *Arts With the Brain in Mind*. Alexandria, VA: Association for Supervision and Curriculum Development.

———. 2008. *Brain-Based Learning: The New Paradigm of Teaching*. 2nd edition. Thousands Oaks, CA: Corwin Press.

Kennedy, Randy. 2006. "Guggenheim Study Suggests Arts Education Benefits Literacy Skills." *The New York Times*, July 27.

Kuta, Katherine. 2003. "And who are you?" *Writing* 25 (5): 30–31.

LaBonty, Jan. 1997. "Poetry in the Classroom: Part I." *The Dragon Lode* 75 (3): 24–26.

LaBonty, Jan, and Kathy Everts Danielson. 2004. "Reading and Writing Poetry in Math." *Reading Horizons* 45 (1): 39–54.

References Cited (cont.)

Landorf, Hilary. 2006. "What's Going on in This Picture? Visual Thinking Strategies and Adult Learning." *New Horizons in Education & Human Resource Development* 20: 28–32.

Lane, Barry. 1992. *After THE END: Teaching and Learning Creative Revision*. Portsmouth, NH: Heinemann.

Lyon, George Ella. 2010. "Where I'm From." Accessed March 2, 2010. http://www.georgeellalyon.com/where.html.

Marzano, Robert J. 2007. *The Art and Science of Teaching: A Comprehensive Framework for Effective Instruction*. Alexandria, VA: ASCD.

McCandless, David. 2010. "David McCandless: The beauty of data visualization." Filmed July 2010, TED video, 18:17. Posted August 2010. http://www.ted.com/talks/david_mccandless_the_beauty_of_data_visualization.html.

McKim, Elizabeth, and Judith W. Steinbergh. 1992. *Beyond Words: Writing Poems With Children: A Guide for Parents and Teachers*. Brookline, MA: Talking Stone Press.

Nascimento, Marcio Luis Ferreira, and Luis Barco. 2007. "How Does Mathematics Look to You?" *Education Canada* 47 (2): 66–70.

National Governors Association Center for Best Practices and Council of Chief State School Officers. 2011. *Common Core State Standards Initiative: The Standards*. Accessed October 10, 2012. http://www.corestandards.org/the-standards.

New, David. 2009. "Listen." National Film Board of Canada video, 6:21. Accessed October 10, 2012. http://www.nfb.ca/film/listen.

Norfolk, Sherry, Jane Stenson, and Diane Williams. 2006. *The Storytelling Classroom*. Westport, CT: Libraries Unlimited.

O'Neill, Cecily. 1995. *Drama Worlds: A Framework for Process Drama*. Portsmouth, NH: Heinemann.

Otten, Samuel. 2011. "Cornered by the Real World: A Defense of Mathematics." *Mathematics Teacher* 105 (1): 20–25.

Perret, Peter, and Janet Fox. 2006. *A Well-Tempered Mind: Using Music to Help Children Listen and Learn*. New York: Dana Press.

Plessinger, Kristin. 2012. *Engaging Learners: Call and Response* (blog), April 16. http://marquetteeducator.wordpress.com/tag/call-and-response/.

President's Committee on the Arts and the Humanities. 2011. "Reinvesting in Arts Education: Winning America's Future Through Creative Schools." Accessed January 2, 2013. http://www.pcah.gov/sites/default/files/PCAH_Reinvesting_4web_0.pdf.

References Cited (*cont.*)

Reed, Stephen K. 2010. *Cognition: Theories and Application*. 8th ed. Belmont, CA: Wadsworth Cengage Learning.

Reeves, Douglas. 2007. "Academics and the Arts." *Educational Leadership* 64 (5): 80–81.

Rhode Island School of Design. 2011. "Gathering STEAM in Rhode Island." Accessed October 10, 2012. http://www.risd.edu/About/News/Gathering_STEAM_in_RI/.

Rinne, Luke, Emma Gregory, Julia Yarmolinskyay, and Mariale Hardiman. 2011. "Why Arts Integration Improves Long-Term Retention of Content." *Mind, Brain, and Education* 5 (2): 89–96.

Skoning, Stacey N. 2008. "Movement in Dance in the Inclusive Classroom." *TEACHING Exceptional Children Plus* 4 (6).

Steen, Lynn Arthur, ed. 1990. *On the Shoulders of Giants: New Approaches to Numeracy*. Washington, DC: National Academies Press.

Strauch-Nelson, Wendy J. 2011. "Book Learning: The Cognitive Potential of Bookmaking." *Teaching Artist Journal* 9 (1): 5–15.

Theodorakou, Kalliopi, and Yannis Zervas. 2003. "The Effects of the Creative Movement Teaching Method and the Traditional Teaching Method on Elementary School Children's Self-Esteem." *Sport, Education and Society* 8 (1): 91–104.

Waters, Sandie H., and Andrew S. Gibbons. 2004. "Design Languages, Notation Systems, and Instructional Technology: A Case Study." *Educational Technology Research & Development* 52 (2): 57–68.

Werner, Linnette Robin. 2001. "Using Dance to Teach Math: The Effects of a Co-Teaching Arts Integration Model on Teacher Practice and Student Learning." PhD diss., University of Minnesota. World Cat (OCLC 50764621).

Wohlberg, Meagan. 2012. "'Don't let the facts spoil a good story': Storyteller Jim Green to release album on Yellowknife's Gold Range." *Slave River Journal* 18.

Zazkis, Rina, and Peter Liljedahl. 2009. *Teaching Mathematics as Storytelling*. Rotterdam, The Netherlands: Sense Publishers.

Zull, James E. 2002. *The Art of Changing the Brain: Enriching Teaching by Exploring the Biology of Learning*. Sterling, VA: Stylus.

Note-Taking Tool for
Observational Assessment

Date _____

Student Name	Comments Made	Questions Asked	General Notes

Arts Integration Assessment Rubric for Mathematics

Student Name _____ Date _____

Skill	Beginning	Developing	Meeting	Exceeding
Demonstrates understanding of mathematical concepts and skills				
Demonstrates understanding of art concepts and skills				
Communicates thinking clearly				
Demonstrates creative thinking				

Individual Observation Form

Student Name _____ Date _____

Shows understanding (Check all that apply)

    _____ Makes representations or notes to understand more fully

    _____ Talks with a peer to understand more fully

    _____ Asks teacher questions to understand more fully

    _____ Helps others to understand

Explains or justifies thinking (Check all that apply)

    _____ Communicates thinking clearly

    _____ Uses art forms, words, symbols, and writing to summarize thinking
(Underline communication forms that apply)

    _____ Uses correct vocabulary

Takes it further (Check all that apply)

    _____ Makes connections to previous learning

    _____ Elaborates on artwork beyond expectations

    _____ Suggests new mathematical connections

    _____ Creates multiple correct responses to task or includes multiple
solution strategies

Printed with the permission of Shell Education (Collins 2012a, 2012b; Dacey 2012a, 2012b, 2012c, 2012d)

Group Observation Form

Student Name _____ Date _____

Use this form to record scores, comments, or both.

Scores: 1—Beginning   2—Developing   3—Meeting   4—Exceeding

Suggests at least one appropriate task solution				
Works cooperatively				
Supports others in their learning				
Communicates clearly, uses correct vocabulary, and builds on the ideas of others				
Provides leadership/ suggestions to group				
Group Members				

Printed with the permission of Shell Education (Collins 2012a, 2012b; Dacey 2012a, 2012b, 2012c, 2012d)

Recommended Resources

Books

Angelou, Maya. 1978. "Still I Rise." In *And Still I Rise*. New York: Random House.

Bunting, Eve. 1993. *Dandelions*. Orlando, FL: First Voyager Books.

Caxton, William. (1484) 2002. *Aesop's Fables*. Reprint, New York: Oxford University Press.

Chute, Marchette. 1957. "The Drinking Fountain." In *Around and About: Rhymes by Marchette Chute*. New York: E. P. Dutton.

Collins, Suzanne. 2010. *The Hunger Games*. New York: Scholastic Press.

Curtis, Christopher Paul. 2012. *The Mighty Miss Malone*. New York: Wendy Lamb Books.

dePaola, Tomie. 1988. "The Secret Place." In *Tomie dePaola's Book of Poems*. New York: Putnam Juvenile.

Dickinson, Emily. 1858. "Autumn." In *The Complete Poems of Emily Dickinson*. New York: Little, Brown and Company.

Grimm, Jacob Ludwing Carl, and Wilhelm Grimm. (1812) 2001. *Hansel and Gretel*. Reprint, New York: North-South Books.

Hughes, Langston. 1994. "April Rain Song." In *The Collected Poems of Langston Hughes*. New York: Vintage Books.

Perrault, Charles. (1697) 1999. *Cinderella*. Reprint, New York: North-South Books.

Roddy, Ruth Mae. 2000. *Minute Monologues for Kids: Contemporary Scene-Study Pieces for Kids*. Rancho Mirage, CA: Dramaline Publications.

Rowling, J. K. 2000. *Harry Potter and the Chamber of Secrets*. New York: Scholastic Paperbacks.

Silverstein, Shel. 1974. "One Inch Tall." In *Where the Sidewalk Ends*. New York: HarperCollins.

Silverstein, Shel. 1981. "Messy Room." In *A Light in the Attic*. New York: HarperCollins.

Soto, Gary. 1995. "Oranges." In *Gary Soto: New and Selected Poems*. San Francisco: Chronicle Books.

Southey, Robert. (1837). 1987. *Goldilocks and the Three Bears*. Reprint, New York: Dodd, Mead, and Company.

Stevens, Chambers. 2009. *Magnificent Monologues for Kids 2: More Kids' Monologues for Every Occasion!* South Pasadena, CA: Sandcastle Publishing.

Tufte, Edward. 2001. *The Visual Display of Quantitative Information*. 2nd ed. Cheshire, CT: Graphic Press

Viorst, Judith. 2009. *Alexander and the Terrible, Horrible, No Good, Very Bad Day*. New York: Atheneum Books for Young Readers.

Recommended Resources (*cont.*)

Whitman, Walt. 1975. "O Captain! My Captain!" In *The Complete Poems*. New York: Penguin Books.

Williams, Vera B. 1982. *A Chair for My Mother*. New York: Morrow/Avon Books.

Periodicals

National Geographic Kids. Tampa, FL: National Wildlife Geographic Society.

Ranger Rick. Reston, VA: National Wildlife Federation.

TIME for Kids. New York: TIME for Kids.

Digital Resources

ArtsEdSearch
http://www.artsedsearch.org/

Solomon LeWitt. "Sol LeWitt A Wall Drawing Retrospective." Accessed January 16, 2013.
http://www.massmoca.org/lewitt/

Visual Resources

Gee's Bend Quilts
http://www.npr.org/templates/story/story.php?storyId=970364

Georges Seurat's *Sunday Afternoon on the Island of La Grande Jatte*
http://www.metmuseum.org/toah/works-of-art/51.112.6

Henri Matisse's *The Goldfish*
http://www.henri-matisse.net/paintings/bga.html

Mary Stevenson Cassatt's *Young Woman in Green, Outdoors In The Sun*
http://www.marycassatt.org/Young-Woman-In-Green-Outdoors-In-The-Sun.html

Pablo Picasso's *Woman in a Blue Hat*
http://www.pablo-ruiz-picasso.net/work-21.php

Robert Seldon Duncanson's *Still Life with Fruits and Nuts*
http://www.nga.gov/press/2012/duncanson.shtm

Toshusai Sharaku's Woodblock Prints
http://www.metmuseum.org/toah/works-of-art/JP2822

Toy Story. Directed by John Lasseter. 1995. Emeryville, CA: Disney Pixar, DVD.

Toy Story 2. Directed by John Lasseter. 1999. Emeryville, CA: Disney Pixar, DVD.

Toy Story 3. Directed by Lee Unkrich. 2010. Emeryville, CA: Disney Pixar, DVD.

Contents of the Digital Resource CD

Page Number	Resource Title	Filename
N/A	Correlation to the Standards	standards.pdf
30	Embodied Movement Brainstorming Guide	embrainstormingguide.pdf embrainstormingguide.doc
31	Embodied Movement Observation Recording Chart	emrecordingchart.pdf emrecordingchart.doc
37	Mirror Moves	mirrormoves.pdf mirrormoves.doc
44	Task Card	taskcard.pdf
45	Experiment Summary	experimentsummary.pdf experimentsummary.doc
53	Pathways	pathways.pdf
54–55	Choreography Planner	choreographyplanner.pdf choreographyplanner.doc
56	Choreography Map	choreographymap.pdf choreographymap.doc
62–63	Six Qualities of Movement Reference Sheet	movementreference.pdf
64	Movement Phrase Graphic Organizer	mpgraphicorganizer.pdf mpgraphicorganizer.doc
75	Sample Museum Director Memo	directormemo.pdf
76	Brainstorming Guide	brainstormingguide.pdf brainstormingguide.doc
81	Detective Script	detectivescript.pdf detectivescript.doc
82	Evidence Chart	evidencechart.pdf evidencechart.doc
88	Gallery Walk Observation Sheet	gallerywalk.pdf gallerywalk.doc
93–95	Scenario Cards	scenariocards.pdf
101	Monologue Example: Cube	monologueexample.pdf
102	Monologue Planner	monologueplanner.pdf monologueplanner.doc
113	Characteristics of Sound	characteristicssound.pdf characteristicssound.doc
114	Music Graph	musicgraph.pdf musicgraph.doc
119	Song Exemplar	songexemplar.pdf

Contents of the Digital Resource CD *(cont.)*

Page Number	Resource Title	Filename
120	Lyric Brainstorming Guide	lyricbrainstorm.pdf
		lyricbrainstorm.doc
121	Chorus and Verses	chorusverses.pdf
		chorusverses.doc
126	Individual Musical Score	musicscore.pdf
		musicscore.doc
131	Call-and-Response Examples	callresponse.pdf
132	Planning Chart for Call-and-Response	callresponseplan.pdf
		callresponseplan.doc
139	Chant Reflection	chantreflection.pdf
		chantreflection.doc
N/A	Musical Score	musicalscore.doc
150	Examples of Dialogue Poems	dialoguepoems.pdf
151	Two Voices Poem Plan	twovoicesplan.pdf
		twovoicesplan.doc
156	Example Poems, Grades K–2	poemsK–2.pdf
157	Example Poems, Grades 3–8	poems3–8.pdf
158	My Fact Poem	factpoem.pdf
		factpoem.doc
159	Fact Poem Planning Guide	factpoemguide.pdf
		factpoemguide.doc
164	Poetry Word List	poetrylist.pdf
		poetrylist.doc
170	Cinquain Samples	cinquainsamples.pdf
171	Word-Count Cinquain Planner	cinquainplanner1.pdf
		cinquainplanner1.doc
172	Parts of Speech Cinquain Planner	cinquainplanner2.pdf
		cinquainplanner2.doc
173	Syllable Cinquain Planner	cinquainplanner3.pdf
		cinquainplanner3.doc
178	Where I'm from Mathematically Examples	wherefrom.pdf
179	Where I'm from Mathematically Planner	wherefromplanner.pdf
		wherefromplanner.doc
191–192	Fox at the Carnival	foxcarnival.pdf
193	Character Development Planner	character.pdf
		character.doc

Contents of the Digital Resource CD (cont.)

Page Number	Resource Title	Filename
194	Math Plot Planner	plot.pdf plot.doc
198–200	Story Starter Cards	startercards.pdf
201–202	Story Starter Organizer	storyorganizer.pdf storyorganizer.doc
208	Tall Math Sentences	tallmath.pdf tallmath.doc
209	Tall Tale Organizer	talltale.pdf talltale.doc
216	What's Been Untold?	untold.pdf untold.doc
221	Story Enders Planner	storyenders.pdf storyenders.doc
232	Storyboard Planner	storyboard.pdf storyboard.doc
240	Circle with 10 Points	10points.pdf
241	Circle with 12 Points	12points.pdf
242	Circle with 23 Points	23points.pdf
248	Data-Collection Planner	dataplanner.pdf dataplanner.doc
249–250	Visual-Representation Planner	visualplanner.pdf visualplanner.doc
256	Sol LeWitt Plan	lewittplan.pdf lewittplan.doc
263	Khipu Numbers	khipu.pdf
264–265	My Khipu	mykhipu.pdf mykhipu.doc

Notes

#51088—Strategies to Integrate the Arts in Mathematics